Dîner du 7 A
Consommé Jardin
Truite Saumonée
Petits Poulets à la
Agneau Rôti
Biscuits
Postkarte
Cartolina Postale
Adresse
POST CARD
FOR CORRESPONDENCE

Secrets of

HANDWRITING ANALYSIS

JACQUI TEW

DK Publishing, Inc.

LONDON, NEW YORK, SYDNEY, DELHI, PARIS, MUNICH, and JOHANNESBURG

First published in the United States of America in 2001 by
DK Publishing, Inc.
95 Madison Avenue, New York, New York, 10016

This book was conceived, designed, and produced by
THE IVY PRESS LIMITED,
The Old Candlemakers, Lewes, East Sussex BN7 2NZ

Art director *Peter Bridgewater*
Editorial director *Sophie Collins*
Designers *Kevin Knight, Jane Lanaway*
Editors *Amy Corzine, Rowan Davies, Sarah Doughty*
Picture researchers *Vanessa Fletcher, Trudi Valter*
Photography *Guy Ryecart*
Illustrations *Sarah Young, Pip Adams, Andrew Kulman, Stephen Raw*
Three-dimensional models *Mark Jamieson*

Cataloging in Publication record is
available from the Library of Congress

ISBN 0-7894-7781-5

Originated and printed by
Hong Kong Graphics and Printing Limited, China

see our complete
catalog at
www.dk.com

CONTENTS

Secrets revealed

Handwriting analysis may reveal certain aspects of people's personalities they had been previously unaware of.

HOW TO USE THIS BOOK

To make *Secrets of Handwriting Analysis* easy to use, it is arranged in three sections. The first introduces basic handwriting movements. This includes an analysis of major aspects and some interpretations that may be applied to them. The second part shows how handwriting analysis is used in the area of work. It begins with an examination of how to put together an analysis. The final section considers the emotions and how they may be observed in handwriting. This part also gives pointers to characteristics of personality and how people fare in relationships. Personal development completes this area.

Warning

To ensure the correct interpretation of handwriting, always check that three different movements which have the same meaning have been made by the writer in the sample analyzed. If you can't find at least three movements that support each conclusion then you run the risk of wrongly attributing certain characteristics to your handwriting subjects.

Basic information

The first part introduces the major handwriting movements and shows how to identify them.

Practical uses
The book goes on to outline the various ways that handwriting analysis can be practically applied.

More detail
Alternative spreads throughout the book give more detailed information on each topic.

Analysis
Some spreads will provide you with the tools to analyze your own emotions and personal relationships.

Introduction

Origins of handwriting analysis
It is remarkable to realize that handwriting analysis first came into existence 2,350 years ago.

Although nobody knows exactly when handwriting analysis first came into existence, the Greek philosopher Aristotle (348–322BC) wrote, "Just as all men do not have the same speech sounds, neither do they all have the same writing."

The Roman historian and biographer Suetonius (c. AD69–150), who wrote accounts of the lives of twelve Roman emperors, analyzed the handwriting of the Emperor Augustus (27BC–AD14). He wrote, "He does not separate the words, nor carry over to the next line any excess letters—this is the writing of a man whose mind is ruled by his heart." In fact, it is known that Emperor Augustus was, indeed, an emotional man. The Chinese painter and philosopher, Kuo Jo Hsu, who lived in the 11th century, wrote that "Handwriting can infallibly show whether it comes from a person who is noble-minded or from one who is vulgar."

The first known book about handwriting analysis was written in the early seventeenth century by an Italian physician named Camillo Baldi. However, serious research did not begin until the nineteenth century. In 1872, two French monks, Abbé Michon and Abbé Flandrin, collected thousands of samples of handwriting and set down an interpretation for each movement. They observed that anyone whose writing was large in size was ambitious. Their research was continued by their students, who discovered that one handwriting movement alone meant nothing. They deemed that it was essential to find three different writing movements with the same meaning before determining that an interpretation was correct. For instance, to confirm an ambitious trait in a personality, at least two other signs would need to be present in the writing, such as rising baselines and heavy pressure.

The spread of analysis

Many Germans went to study with these French monks and subsequently developed a scientific approach to analyzing handwriting. Handwriting analysis spread to Germany in this manner and then to the rest of Europe. Taught in universities, it was used widely as part of employment selection before the Second World War. It spread to the United States at the beginning of the twentieth century.

Today there is renewed interest in handwriting analysis. There are many ways in which it can be applied and it continues to be used to determine the suitability of job applicants. This is because someone's handwriting can tell us a great deal about them, helping us to assess their character and potential.

UNDERSTANDING
THE BASICS

There are many ways to analyze handwriting. To be accurate, it is important to follow two vital guidelines. First, it is essential to detect the signs or movements present in the handwriting correctly. To help you decide what movements are present, take a pen that has run out of ink and trace over the writing of the sample to be analyzed. Doing this for a couple of minutes will assist you in your observations. The second crucial guideline is to find sufficient supporting evidence from other signs that have the same interpretation. At first, you may wish to make a quick assessment. To do this, go to page 218, where you will find that different movements illustrate and support each interpretation. If the writing sample contains three different movements with the same meaning, you will know that your evaluation is correct.

The Equipment Needed

Very few tools
With a writing sample and just a few pieces of equipment, you will be ready to start.

The main requirement for assessing someone's character using handwriting analysis is a sample of their handwriting. The science of handwriting analysis involves the appraisal of many aspects of the writing sample in order to make an evaluation of the writer's character.

Some information about the writer is also required because handwriting analysis cannot determine certain factors, for example age, gender, and nationality. The handwriting analyst also needs to know whether the writer's right or left hand has been used, and also of any physical or educational difficulties the writer may have, such as arthritis, dyslexia, a broken arm, and so on. The handwriting analyst should be aware of the purpose of the analysis, i.e., whether the writer wants to find a new career, or a compatible partner.

The analyst's tool kit

The handwriting analyst's tool kit for analyzing writing might also include a magnifying glass, a dead pen, a ruler, and a pencil. A professional analyst may also use a protractor to determine the exact angle of the writing's slant and some carbon paper. Pressure is difficult to measure, but placing a couple of sheets of carbon paper between three plain pieces of paper on which the writer writes will enable you to see the amount of indentation made by the pen into the paper. An analyst also needs a movement worksheet on which to record a description of the writer's handwriting movements. The sample needs to be written on a plain piece of paper that rests on a pad of paper, or a magazine, which is set on a steady, immoveable writing desk or surface. Ideally, the writer should use a pen of his own choice, but do make a note on your movement worksheet if the individual has no particular preference.

The content of the sample is immaterial so long as its text is written spontaneously—that is to say, it must not be copied from something else. When finished, the writer is asked to sign their normal signature at the bottom of the handwriting sample.

Movement Worksheet

This is used to describe each writing movement present in the writing sample:

- Size
- Zones
- Slant
- Width
- Connectedness
- Line spacing
- Word spacing
- Rhythm
- Regularity
- Style
- Baselines
- Pressure
- Thickness of pen stroke
- Letter forms
- Margins

BALANCE

Balanced writing can be seen where the movements look mainly in proportion. Because we are humans rather than robots, nobody can produce perfectly symmetrical writing spontaneously with a pen. However, balanced writing can show a person who has found a satisfactory way to live their life, which takes into account both work and the pursuit of pleasure. Balanced writing can be observed in many different ways, just as there are various approaches and attitudes to life. When a sample emphasizes particular features, the writer has chosen specific priorities in their life.

Slightly dominant middle zone

Zones are well balanced

Practical

In this sample, the zones (see pages 24–25) are fairly well balanced, with the middle zone being slightly dominant showing an interest in people and practicality. The spacing is also fairly well balanced indicating that the writer has the ability to know when to speak and when to listen.

Aujourd'hui, maman
hier, je ne sais pas.
de l'asile : « Mère déc
demain. Sentiments
veut rien dire. Cl

CAMUS, Albert   L'E

True silence is the rest of the mind, it is to the spirit what sleep is to the body, nourishment and refreshment.

William Penn.

ADVENTUROUS SAMPLE

Rightward slant

Broad width

Spacing is well balanced

morte. On peut-être
i reçu un télégramme
e. Enterrement
ingués. ⚹ Cela ne
it peut-être hier.

nger

PRACTICAL SAMPLE

Adventurous

In this sample, there is a right slant and broad width in the writing, indicating a person who is keen for adventure, spontaneous, and enjoys listening to new ideas. As this writer is willing to take risks, some ideas will bring her tremendous happiness, while others will cause her sadness or frustration.

Size • 1

Size is revealing

Large or small? Both sizes of writing reveal good points.

The size of our writing indicates the way we see ourselves and how we rate our self-image. It also provides a pointer to our hopes and dreams. Whether we achieve our goals depends on other factors in the writing such as the pressure exerted, which tells us whether we have sufficient energy to achieve our ambitions.

The balance

When the overall height of the writing is pleasing to look at, the letters are probably of an average size. An average size shows a writer with a sense of proportion. This allows an inner harmony to blend with a disciplined personality. Writers who use medium-sized letters enjoy routine and tradition. They tend to be realistic and practical, mixing easily into any situation or group, and adapting when changes are needed.

Letters that are too large may indicate a degree of compensation— the writer may be showing more confidence than she actually feels inside. This can be a great asset in instances where shy people may have to give speeches to huge audiences: the enlarged size shows how they boost their courage to deliver a confident and successful presentation.

When the writing size is minute, these writers tend to have excellent concentration and will gain pleasure from an in-depth study of any topic in which they are interested. They can be a valuable asset to employers who are looking for somebody to do thorough preparatory research.

How to judge size

Size is one of the movements that is easily changeable. Someone whose writing is normally large might have to make their script smaller to fit the whole message on the paper available, perhaps a postcard, for instance. In order to assess the true size therefore, it is wise to give the writer a sheet of standard-sized paper. This allows the natural, true size of the writing to emerge freely.

Make sure that the writer has enough paper on which to write normally, and enough text to make sure that he lapses into his ordinary style while writing. This ensures that his subconscious and natural personality are revealed.

Size: The Key

Large writing indicates an individual with initiative, liveliness, enthusiasm, generosity, imagination, vigor, and the ability to make emotional judgements. Small-sized writing indicates an individual with good concentration, precision, thoroughness, modesty, and intensity.

SIZE • 2

The size of someone's writing can create an optical illusion for the lay reader with no graphological knowledge. Large writing may give the reader the impression that the writer is a tall person, when the writer may actually be short. The size of our writing shows how we behave in a frightening situation. After all, at some stage we all face fear in our lives. The larger its size, the more extrovert will be our reaction; and the smaller the size, the more we will take time to be cautious and ponder the options before taking action. Both means of coping can be successful, because it is the amount of rhythm we have that determines how well we cope with fear.

Harmony

This writer has a lot of movements that are in harmony. The small size, the mainly connected letters, and wide word spacing show that he has good concentration, a good eye for detail, and on the whole prefers to work quietly on his own. The line spacing may look close, but it is in fact in balance with the rest of his style.

Connected letters

Wide word spacing

"Some people think football.
I don't like that attitude
more ~~in~~ serious than that."

gh

I'd like to be a teabag,
And stay at home all day –
And talk to other teabags
In a teabag sort of way. . . .

Slight
left
slant

Close word
spacing

SOCIABILITY SAMPLE

Sociability

The small size seen in this writing, along with the legibility, connected letters, and close word spacing shows that the writer enjoys company and she is keen to communicate clearly. The slight slant to the left indicates her loyalty to others.

a matter of life and death.
...an assure them it is much
Shankly, P 918 / 69

HARMONY SAMPLE

Size • 3

The size factor
*Size alone cannot reveal
whether someone is detail-oriented
or has a broader view of life.*

The overall size of our writing is
primarily an indicator of how
confident we feel about ourselves.
However, while the size of our writing is
a feature that is often noticed instantly, it
can be misleading. Large writing may
be one of the signs of ambition, but
other features indicate how far those
ambitions are likely to be achieved.
This can be assessed by examining the
combination of writing movements on
the page. The amount of pressure used
in pressing pen to paper shows the
energy available to the writer, so
people who write with adequate

pressure as well as with large size will
probably achieve their goals. However,
so will an individual with small writing
who also uses heavy pressure. Those
with large writing may reach their
goals first, but writers with small and
large writing can both succeed.

People with small-sized writing are
often modest. This feature of their
personality, while they may not
recognize it, gives them the ability to
assess themselves realistically, which
allows them to accept themselves at
their true worth more easily.

Positive application

People with large writing tend to be
enthusiastic and ambitious, and to have
a broad outlook on life. They enjoy
being able to visualize future projects
on a large scale, preferring to leave
the small details to others. They often
project an air of self-confidence and
frequently offer to try out new ideas.
People with small writing, on the other
hand, tend to love detail, which makes
them a valuable asset for tasks where

a particularly thorough approach is required. They usually have an in-depth interest in whatever they are doing and they enjoy problem solving. Individuals with small writing are usually observant and attentive to small things, so are useful when there is an exacting task to be carried out.

A analyst's interpretation of someone's writing can be correct only when there are three different movements in the writing that carry the same meaning. For instance, while people with small writing tend to have sustained concentration, love detail, and be very thorough, this is not always the case. Someone who writes each letter separately within a word will prefer to do lots of different things that require only short spans of attention, and so, even if the person's writing is small, she may not be capable of sustained concentration. Someone with large writing may work well with someone with small writing: the former can articulate an overall vision while the latter attends to the detail.

SIZE • 4

When talking about size, it is important to distinguish between the absolute size and the relative size. The absolute size takes into account the measurement from the top of ascenders (such as the top stroke of the letter "h") to the bottom of descenders (such as the tail of the letter "g"), while the relative size applies to each individual zone. The absolute size can be changed fairly easily by doing so consciously, but the individual zones are determined by the unconscious and, therefore, cannot be altered at will. Although these two samples are both of an average absolute size, they may look different because one has a dominant middle zone and the other has a small middle zone.

Horizontal mingling

Clear line space

Organizational

On taking a closer look at the writing with a predominantly small middle zone, it can be seen that the letters in this area vary in size, showing a versatile writer who likes to take an analytical approach to life. He is happiest when he can base his answers on known facts.

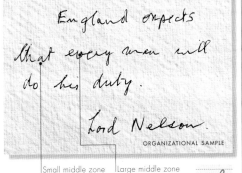

England expects that every man will do his duty.

Lord Nelson.

ORGANIZATIONAL SAMPLE

Small middle zone · Large middle zone

gh

et 3,000 hits, rnoon on Aaron.

ANALYTICAL SAMPLE

Dominant middle zone

Analytical

The sample with the dominant middle zone has little fluctuation in the size. With close word spacing and good line spacing, this writer enjoys planning and organizing a full social life. He may well enjoy team activities and occasions where there is plenty of time to chat.

Zones •1

Your three zones

How and where we choose to emphasize our zones displays aspects of our individuality.

In graphological terms, handwriting can be divided vertically into three parts. Each individual part is called a zone. Three zones go together to make the absolute size. Each zone has a particular significance. The upper zone indicates our ideals and hopes, our spiritual aspirations, and our ethics. The middle zone shows how we relate to others and fit in with everyday life, and the lower zone reflects the depth of our feelings and our instinctual drives. The different sizes in the zones are exclusive to each one of us.

The balance

Balanced zones indicate an equilibrium of interest in all aspects of life. When there is also a healthy mix of angles and curves to be found in the writing, these individuals will use their available resources wisely.

Often one zone will be found to be larger, thus creating a weaker zone elsewhere. This simply means that the writer has a stronger interest in the area of the dominant zone. For instance, if there is a prominent upper zone, the writer may have great ambitions, be fascinated by life-after-death experiences, or be highly ethical. Perhaps the lower zone becomes weaker as a result. This means their interests and energy are directed toward mental pursuits rather than unconscious drives.

How to judge zones

There is more than one view as to what constitutes balanced zones. In some countries, when children are taught to write they are instructed to make each individual zone the same height. In other countries, the upper and lower zones are extended, making them each twice the size of the middle zone. For this reason it is useful to ask the writer how they were taught to make the individual zones.

When measuring the height of each individual zone, it is wise to take about ten different measurements and make a note of them. Observe the average size of the zone, and then determine whether the variation in letter size is larger than average. When this is the case, the writer suffers from a lack of harmony in this area. Remember—handwriting analysis is based on each writer's individual variations.

Zones: The Key

The dominant upper zone indicates an individual with high ideals, hopes, and aspirations; the dominant middle zone indicates an individual who is sociable, practical, and lives for the present; the dominant lower zone indicates an individual with instinctual and physical drives, including a depth of interest in personal security.

ZONES • 2

Zones give a wealth of information to the analyst. Measuring and assessing the different sizes of each individual zone reveals the balance and the conflict, strengths, and fears which are to be found in each area of the writer's personality. Although loops in the zones indicate ideas or dreams, they have totally different applications according to the zone in which they appear. In the upper zone, loops indicate our longing to achieve goals, while in the lower zone they reveal a need for security and stability.

Idealistic

A dominant upper zone is rare. This writer has high ideals and aspirations. It may be difficult for him to find people of his caliber. His expectations are high and he is willing to put in a lot of hard work to achieve his goals. Unfortunately, in the world of today when many people are more interested in getting a job done quickly, this could be frustrating for this writer, who would like to take his time to do a good job. He is far-sighted and may be able to visualize large-scale projects in his mind before they reach the drawingboard.

Dominant upper zone

Varying middle zone

When you have work to do & you don't want to do it, decide what really needs to be done and what can wait. Unknown

IDEALISTIC SAMPLE

> When you have ~~to~~ work to do you don't want to do it, decide what really needs to be done and what can wait. Upkown.

SOCIABLE SAMPLE

Virtually no upper zone

Dominant middle zone

Sociable

In contrast, this writer has virtually no upper zone. However, she has a dominant middle zone. For her, living for today and enjoying a good social life are important. Although she is happy to face the future, she has not attached a great deal of importance to planning her life in the long term. The broad letters show that she has an open mind and is willing to listen to new ideas.

> The Owl and the Pussycat
> went to sea,
> In a beautiful pea-green boat.
> They took some honey and
> plenty of money.
> Wrapped up in a five pound
> note.

ANALYTICAL SAMPLE

Dominant lower zone

Mingling lines

Analytical

This writer has a dominant lower zone which indicates that she likes to get to the bottom of things. To her, it is important to find out the cause of a problem, or to discover all the facts that are relevant to a project. Her wide word spacing indicates that she enjoys in-depth one-to-one chats, and she is keen to know what makes the other person tick. She has a lovely sense of humor and the connected letters in her writing show that she has a logical approach to life.

Zones • 3

Each zone is important
*Your middle zone will reveal,
among other things, whether or not
you enjoy socializing at parties*

Zones give a unique view of where a writer's interests and energies are most strongly centered. The zone emphasized shows not only in which field the writer feels most confident, but also discloses what is going on behind the mask that most of us wear in everyday life.

When the middle zone is slightly smaller and the upper and lower zones are slightly larger, with some fluctuation in height of the strokes within each particular zone, these writers strive for harmony. They do not like to stretch themselves beyond what they know they can achieve. Choosing comfortably attainable goals in this way gives them a feeling of happiness and contentment. These individuals often have unassuming personalities.

Positive application

The more dominant the upper zone, the more idealistic the writer tends to be. Such people are high-minded, and can be visionaries. A dominant middle zone indicates people who live very much in the present. They enjoy socializing, and, especially if the space between the words is also close, they are ready for a party at any time.

Individuals who produce a dominant lower zone and small writing tend to be good observers. This is because, as this signifies, they have their feet firmly on the ground and are not consumed by ego. Sometimes one zone can be so prominent that the other two zones become virtually nonexistent. Writers who do this put all of their energies into one area of life.

When there is a large variation of letter size within any one zone, it indicates conflict in the area signified by the zone. In the upper zone this could mean that someone has great aspirations, but that their goals are not attainable. Perhaps the individual has had to choose between having a family and following a demanding career. Whichever choice has been made, and whatever path has been followed, the writer may later wish a different one had been taken.

A large size variation in the middle zone indicates that these writers exude confidence and are very articulate when they are talking about a topic of which they are knowledgeable. They will want to shrink into the background and will become very quiet, however, when they are uncertain about the accuracy of their facts.

Large strokes in the lower zone or large fluctuation in letter size in this region show that these writers will have yearnings for security and yet also want to take risks.

ZONES • 4

If one analyzes samples of teenagers' handwriting, one often finds that the girls' samples have a dominant middle zone. This indicates their enjoyment of socializing, and the importance they place on friends and making time for a chat. On the other hand, samples of teenage boys' handwriting often show dominant upper and lower zones. These indicate their love of sports and enjoyment of physical activity. Balanced zones are usually found in the writing of mature adults who have experienced life in many ways and have enjoyed good times, but have also dealt with some difficult challenges.

Friendly

The writer of this sample has a lot of positive qualities. Garlands and roundedness show a friendly and empathetic personality. The different sizes in the middle zone indicate flexibility: look at the different sizes of the letter "o," or the "bu" of "but." There is some flowing rhythm present, suggesting that the writer is contented with life. The well-spaced layout shows that the writer fits easily into society.

Large "o"

Small "o"

Friends do not live in harmony merely, as some say, but in melody.

Henry David Thoreau (1817–1862)

FRIENDLY SAMPLE

Concentration

This writer has fairly large upper and lower zones; as a result, the middle zone is rather small. This kind of writing is often produced by certain sorts of men who give a lot of attention to their work and also to sports, for which they have plenty of enthusiasm. The result is that they do not have much energy left in the social zone. For example, this sample suggests that the writer prefers an in-depth discussion with one person at a time to socializing in group situations.

Large upper and lower zones

Small middle zone

In family life, Love is the oil that eases friction, the cement that binds closer together, and the music that brings harmony. General Eva Burrows.

CONCENTRATION SAMPLE

Versatility

This fascinating sample shows great variation in the size of the letters in the middle zone. Note the size of the letter "o" on each of the four occasions that it is written. The writer is a versatile person who can do many things. She is also full of ideas.

Large "o"   Small "o"

We can only learn to love by loving.

VERSATILITY SAMPLE

Slant • 1

Slant is not consistent
The slant of your writing can change; it may alter, for example, when you fall in love.

People sometimes say they write in various different ways. But when one sees the styles that are presented for analysis, it is often merely the slope of the writing that has changed. As the slant is an expression of emotion, it is an easily changeable feature in the handwriting and may alter depending on the circumstances of the individual at the time of writing.

Sometimes, when people fall passionately in love, they may find that their writing slopes more to the right. But when an activity demands a great deal of concentration, for example the writing of a letter about something that is important, the writer will notice that

their writing becomes steadily more upright as common sense gradually becomes the focus of their thoughts.

There is no right or wrong slant. Extroverted people tend to write with a slope to the right, reaching out toward people, while others of a more introverted nature lean toward the left, away from others.

The balance

Those who allow themselves to have some emotion, but do not let feelings rule their lives may produce writing that is upright, or slopes slightly to the right or to the left. These writers take mainly logical decisions. However, in appropriate situations they will allow emotional options to be taken into consideration before coming to the solution that suits their circumstances.

The upright slant denotes a commonsense and realistic approach to life. People who write in this way will choose the most sensible way ahead and one that is best on a practical level for themselves.

How to judge slant

Few people have handwriting that is always absolutely upright in its trajectory. If it is, it indicates that the writer has enormous self-discipline. Writing that always has a forward inclination is known as a right slant. When the angle of the writing slopes backward all the time, it is called a left slant.

When a mixed slant is present, the writing will slope both to the right and to the left. Upright strokes may be seen in the handwriting as well. Writing which slants all one way may also produce a variety of angles.

Slant: The Key

A right slant indicates an individual who is warm-hearted, adventurous, sociable, enthusiastic, courageous, and spontaneous. A left slant indicates someone who is loyal, cautious, secretive, reflective, and able to make decisions based on past experiences. An upright slant indicates a person who is practical, level-headed, and has common sense and a logical approach. A mixed slant indicates an individual who has artistic ability, is flexible, and loves variety.

SLANT · 2

While someone can easily change the slant of their handwriting for a short time, it is not possible for individuals to write for long with a slant that masks their feelings. Getting someone to write a long sample for analysis on an 8½ x 11 inch sheet of writing paper will help you to gain an accurate picture of the writer's emotions. It is generally true to say that, when we start to write, we may be conscious of our writing's appearance, but once we start to concentrate on the content of the text, our pens begin to move in time with the rhythm of our real emotions so that our personalities are revealed.

Empathy

This sample is written by a warm-hearted and friendly person. Although she has a right slant, there are also a lot of connected letters showing that while she is an empathetic person, she can also use logic when it is appropriate to do so. The sharp strokes in her writing indicate that she is also sensitive. However, the rigidity in her rhythm indicates that she would rather not wear her heart on her sleeve.

Right slant

Connected letters

EMPATHY SAMPLE

_tt_

SECRETS OF HANDWRITING ANALYSIS

Compassion

The right slant and sharpness that are produced by this writer are expressions of his compassion for others. The connected letters convey his logical approach and determination to keep going in the face of difficulty.

Connected letters

Right slant

> Ich lebe nun schon 42 Jahre in England lein immer noch Deutsch aber fühle mich himmlisch wohl in diesem Land.

COMPASSION SAMPLE

Practicality

An upright slant shows a person who is practical and uses common sense. The writer in this sample has a large middle zone, which is an indicator of being down-to-earth and sensible. With her legible writing style and clear spacing, it is apparent that she is a good organizer.

Legible letters   Clear style

> Cet homme a acheté quatre-vingt-un chevaux et soixante-dix vaches.

PRACTICALITY SAMPLE

Slant • 3

Slant may be taught
The way someone is taught to write at school will probably differ from their natural writing style.

S lant is one of the graphic elements that is taught differently in schools, depending upon the handwriting style of the country concerned. The precise writing style that has been learned will also depend on the age of the writer.

In Britain, the Vere Foster method of handwriting was taught until shortly after the Second World War. This style produced a rightward slant with loops in letters such as the "l" and "h"; most of the letters within each word were joined together. The Marion Richardson technique superseded the Vere Foster method. This style has an upright slant with single straight strokes for such letters as "l" and "h," and incomplete loops for letters such as "g" and "y." In France, a rightward slant is part of the country's copybook style, as it also is in the United States. However, in Germany an upright slant is more usual.

While you may have been taught to write with a particular slant you have unconsciously decided, as an adult, upon your own style of writing. It is fascinating to see people who write the text of their message with a slant that slopes one way and then sign their names with a slant that goes in the opposite direction. The slant in the text shows how the individual would like to be viewed, but the signature exposes the real emotions of the writer.

Positive application

Individuals with a slope to the right tend to be warm-hearted and demonstrative in showing their love toward others. They will often make emotional choices rather than rational decisions. They tend to enjoy being with people and to be sympathetic to the feelings of others.

When the writing slopes backward, it often means that these individuals prefer to keep their feelings to themselves. They probably have one or two very close friends and are usually intensely loyal to those whom they love.

People with a mixed slant are often creative and enjoy having lots of diverse projects to work on at the same time. Variety is important in the lives of those whose writing angle covers a selection of different directions.

Those who have an upright slant are good to have around in a crisis. They are able to remain cool and calm, and make rational decisions even when they are under a lot of stress.

The slant of our handwriting indicates how we express our emotions. It has nothing to do with happiness, which is available to everyone, whatever the slant of their writing. Balance and harmony may be observed in writing that is rhythmic and consistent.

SLANT • 4

A slant that leans heavily to the right may look superficially different from one that leans heavily to the left, but both these individuals will have strong and passionate emotions. They will both allow their feelings to determine how decisions are made. Writers with a marked slant in either direction will often be driven to action because they will feel this is the best way forward. This can be a great asset in times of challenge when communities need to work together to deal with crises like floods.

Emotional

In this sample the flow of the writing is lively and natural. The writer appears to have a mainly right slant. However, there are some letters that are at almost ninety degrees and

there is even the rare sight of a left slant. This shows that the writer has a full range of emotions. The spontaneity and broad width of the writing reflect her love of travel, new

experiences, and making the most of life. This sample's clear word and line spacing shows that she can think on her feet and change her priorities as her situation changes.

Rare left slant

If you talk about yourse you are boring. If you talk he'll think you're a gossip about him, he'll think you conversationalist.

38

"Let's build a den!"
"You go and get the sticks and stones, and I'll think of a name for it."

EMPATHY SAMPLE

The lower-to-upper-zone gap is narrow

Slight leftward slant

Empathy

This slant can be deceptive. It appears to be upright; however, on closer inspection, one may see that it has a slight slope to the left. This indicates that the writer is a practical person. The prevailing garland letter forms show that she is empathetic, a good listener, and someone with common sense. Although the writing lines appear to be well spaced, the gap between some lower zones and the upper zones of the following lines is in fact very narrow, with some letters almost clashing.

he'll think
about others,
If you talk
a brilliant

Right slant

tt

EMOTIONAL SAMPLE

Width • 1

un

How to judge width
*Broad width occurs when the horizontal
width of letters exceeds the vertical
height of the letters.*

The width of the letters in a sample of writing indicates a person's approach to life. The broader the writing, the more inclined the writer is to be open to new ideas and to take the risk of trying out new concepts.

Broadness in writing indicates people who are willing to go forward and tackle whatever the future may hold. Whether they are facing unpleasant stressful situations or pioneering new and unexplored frontiers in their own lives, their ability to be spontaneous, and to listen and remain cheerful while trying out untested ideas, can be a great asset in overcoming interim hazards and despondency. They also make extremely good friends.

Narrow writing is found in those who are single-minded and prefer to work within a set framework of known and approved theories. These writers can be an asset in areas such as scientific research, where experiments must be carried out by following a rigorously predetermined formula.

Balance

Those whose writing is just slightly wide, slightly narrow, or of average width have a balanced approach to life. Sometimes they will be open-minded, but on other occasions they will have firm views that they do not wish to change.

The wider the writing, the more the writer is willing to take misguided risks. When the width becomes too narrow, the writer's determination may, on occasion, become tunnel vision.

How to judge width

The lower case "u" is one of the letters most frequently used to establish the width of writing. Look at the two vertical lines that make up this letter and then observe the horizontal space between the two vertical lines. Determine whether the greater length is horizontal or vertical. Broad writing is described as writing whose horizontal width is greater than its vertical width. When the vertical width is greater than the horizontal width, the writing is said to be narrow.

The lower case "n" is also used to determine width in handwriting, but it is a good idea to note that the shape of this letter can be easily misinterpreted, so it needs careful consideration. Sometimes the two downstrokes are written at angles that meet each other at the top rather than as parallel lines with a joining stroke.

Width: The Key

Broad writing indicates an individual who is enthusiastic, resourceful, friendly, and flexible, with an enterprising nature, and a laid-back approach. Narrow writing indicates an individual who has good concentration and is diligent, tenacious, committed, economical, and careful.

WIDTH • 2

Width is an interesting movement because it enables the analyst to assess balance in a more subtle way. Those who write with an average width will enjoy equilibrium in their lives most of the time. People with narrow width will perceive balance in a different way. They will focus all their concentration on the task at hand and only when this is complete will they take time to relax and recuperate, thus redressing the imbalance in their lives, which has been caused by their concentration on one thing.

Single-Mindedness

In this example of narrow width, it is interesting to note that nearly all the letters are narrow. This shows someone who likes to set a target and then give their undivided attention to achieving their goal. The writer is determined, and the wide spaces between the words indicate that he prefers to work either alone or in the company of one other person.

Narrow width

Inferiors revolt in order that they may be equal, and equals that they may be superior. Such is the state of mind which creates revolutions. Aristotle.

SINGLE-MINDEDNESS SAMPLE

n

Good Company

With broad width and a slant to the right, this writer is good company and enjoys a wealth of different interests. She is open to new ideas and willing to enhance her knowledge by looking at fresh ways of approaching things.

> What i Cannot love, i Overlook.
> Is that real friendship?
>
> Anaïs Nin

GOOD COMPANY SAMPLE

Right slant

Broad width   Narrow width

Willingness to Learn

This writer displays both narrowness and broadness, and some of her letter formations are narrow at the top of the middle zone and wide when they reach the baseline. She is keen to both learn and listen to new ideas, and has the single-mindedness that is required to persevere until she reaches her goal.

> 3 rules of work 1
> out of clutter, find simplicity
> 2 From discord find harmony
> 3 In the middle of difficulty
> lies opportunity
>
> Author Albert Einstein

WILLINGNESS TO LEARN SAMPLE

Width • 3

Width reflects personality
*Both broad and narrow writing styles
can be indicative of some positive
personality traits.*

Broad writing is an amplification of a personality. Broad writers tend to be chatty and easygoing, and allow themselves a lot of freedom. They enjoy socializing and may be good at the kind of "small talk" required to make an impact on business and social functions. People with narrow writing prefer situations where they can talk in depth about one subject. Narrowness indicates a restriction of the writing movement. When people are overstressed, a narrow element is often found in their writing. To produce narrow writing all the time requires rigorous self-discipline and places a constant strain on the personality.

Positive application

For those who have chosen to devote their time to achieving a goal—athletic success, for example—narrow writing could be a positive feature. It shows traits which help them to stay on target to accomplish their dream. On the other hand, those who are working in an industry where it is important to know what is going on in many different areas would be better off with broad handwriting traits. Broad writing reveals the ability to try new ventures and pioneer untested fields.

Society needs both people with very broad writing, so that advances can be made more speedily, and those with extremely narrow writing, so that a single-minded and thorough examination can be made when it is required. There are great positive benefits to having very wide or very narrow writing.

It has to be for each of us to decide if it is more acceptable to produce a balanced writing that is slightly narrow or slightly wide, or the more positive extremes of broad or narrow writing at each end of the scale. Of course, while there are positive traits for both broad and narrow writing, the more unbalanced the writing either way, the more negative interpretations will also apply.

It is only when all the writing movements are analyzed as a whole that the kind of personality the writer has may be determined. For example, when the two vertical points of the letter "n" join in a point at the top, they show extreme narrowness in approach or character, but then they broaden out and end up far apart on the baseline. This indicates people who would like to be seen as open and ready to listen, but underneath this facade they are actually narrow-minded. Positively interpreted, this shows tact; but it may also denote people who agree to things that they have no intention of doing.

WIDTH · 4

Handwriting width can indicate the different ways in which people like to learn. Writers with broad width enjoy learning by gathering a general overview of a new subject. Those who have narrow writing prefer to concentrate on one area and delve deeply into the foundations or history of a project so that they can gather all the possible facts within a particular field. This in-depth approach gives these people the feeling of inner confidence that they have understood and can properly apply their new-found knowledge.

One "n" form

La bie n'est pas t
vous ne parlez pas d
Les garsons ne coups
demain la bes.

n

Exercise is bunk. If you are healthy, you
don't need it; if you are sick you shouldn't
take it.

       Attributed to Henry Ford, American car manufacturer.
                  1863 – 1947.

Broad width

NEW IDEAS SAMPLE

Average width

Open to New Ideas

Width can be difficult to judge correctly, especially when the middle zone letters are small. In this example, where the upper and lower zones are dominant, the middle zone is instantly recognizable as the weak zone. On careful inspection, it can be seen that the width is mainly average, with some wider letters in the middle zone. This writer is open to new ideas, and with her right slant and no right margin, she is always keen to explore unknown territory.

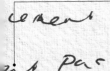

Second "n" form

Diversity of Interest

Broadness in writing shows a diversity of interests. This writer's sample shows that, as well as having broadness, the writing is disconnected. A right slant indicates her fascination for a host of different activities and views. Note that, each time she writes the letter "n," its style varies, which indicates enhanced creativity.

DIVERSITY SAMPLE

Connected • 1

fecit

Making connections

There is a social significance to the number of letters connected in each piece of writing.

The number of letters joined together within each word indicates the kinds of thought processes and mental attitudes someone has. People who connect their letters use logic in all situations, and are interested in facts.

There is also a social significance to the number of letters that we choose to connect. The more we join letters together, the more we enjoy mixing with other people and socializing in groups.

Unconnected letters reflect an imaginative mind. The writer who does not join letters together flourishes in a "think tank" type of situation. It also shows the ability of a writer to cope with several tasks at once. People who

do not join their letters together thrive on variety, which also allows them to use their concentration to its full potential.

The balance

When three or four letters are joined together before a break within words, this indicates a balance between connected and disconnected writing. These individuals may have many intuitive ideas and also the ability to apply logic to find out which of their concepts can be turned into reality.

How to judge connectedness

When all letters are joined together in a word, the writing is very connected. Even if a writer breaks the flow to stop and dot an "i" or cross a "t," the writing is still known as connected writing.

When every letter is an entity on its own within a word, this is known as disconnectedness. Straightforward disconnectedness is easy to see, as the letters are written separately. However, two letters which touch each other but are not actually joined may indicate false connectedness. This is found in many writing samples where the text is clear and legible. It means that these writers are articulate when delivering factual information. They have difficulty revealing their inner feelings, however, and prefer other people to guess when they need a gentle approach or are feeling delicate.

Air strokes—which, as their name indicates, occur in the air and therefore do not leave a mark on the paper—are also counted as connected strokes. This is because, although the pen has come off the paper, it has continued to move in the same direction and maintains the same course when the ink trail returns to the paper. Writers who use air strokes may be tired, or they may have minds that work faster than their pens.

Connections: The Key

Connected writing indicates logical thinking, a preference for doing one task at a time, and problem solving. Disconnected writing indicates intuition, imagination, plenty of ideas, and concentration in short bursts.

CONNECTED • 2

A single writing movement on its own does not have any meaning; to make an accurate reading you will need to observe at least two movements that indicate the same quality or personality trait. Two movements that suggest imagination are disconnected writing and loops in the upper zone. People whose writing displays these characteristics will have many ideas, while those who also have large writing will be able to visualize future large-scale projects. They may work well with people who have connected writing and no loops, since they have a logical approach and can plan how to turn dreams into reality.

Logical

This sample shows a healthy use of connected letters. There are occasional gaps where the writer has taken the pen off the paper between two letters; this indicates that the writer allows intuitive ideas to filter through and to be used when appropriate. On the whole, this writer likes a logical approach to life. On occasion, she may get carried away with her own interests, which could result in losing all sense of time; her concentration is fully absorbed in the pursuit of the moment.

Occasional gap

" When one door another opens; bu at the closed door the one which ha

Liebe Mary!

Wir freuen uns auf dein Kommen.
Natürlich werden wir dich vom
Flughafen abholen. Du
mußt uns nur die genaue
Ankunftszeit schreiben.

Bis bald, Dein Wulf

CREATIVITY
SAMPLE

Disconnection
between "u" and "a"

Disconnection
between "m" and "a"

Creativity

This writing appears very connected and indeed there are some words where every letter is joined with others, and yet the odd word contains quite a number of disconnected letters. This writer is a fast and creative thinker who likes to get to the root of a problem and then find a long-term solution. The irregularity and thin pen stroke show that he has plenty of original thoughts and ideas.

happiness closes,

often we look so long

that we do not see

opened for us,"

Helen Keller.

Occasional gap

LOGICAL SAMPLE

Connected • 3

Horizontal mingling

Close inspection is required in order to establish the exact extent of connectedness.

It is sometimes easy to form a superficial impression as to whether the writing is generally connected or disconnected. As we have seen, on closer inspection, we may find that letters are touching, but not actually joined together. This false connectedness is sometimes called "horizontal mingling."

Sometimes we can mistake disconnected letters for writing that has been "printed." Disconnected writing will have uneven spaces between the letters, while printing will have a set pattern. It can be easier to recognize printing when the writing appears in capital letters. As disconnected writing is slower to produce than connected writing, those who have to print words as part of their job will often unwittingly join letters together.

Sometimes you may come across disconnected letters. If these are in a sample where letters are normally joined together in a word, this can indicate that the individual was under a lot of stress at the time of writing. When normal life resumes, the gaps between the letters will also disappear.

Positive application

Those who like to join their letters usually stop to cross the "t" and dot the "i." These breaks allow the writer to pause and reflect. When there are absolutely no breaks between letters, it indicates that individuals like to do one task at a time and preferably without being disturbed. They may well enjoy variety but they prefer just to concentrate on the task in hand.

Writing that is naturally disconnected shows individuals who are often very imaginative and have a wealth of new ideas. They are usually intuitive and know what others are thinking. Letters that are all written separately can even be a sign of genius.

Rhythm is more difficult to produce in writing that is disconnected. People who are able to combine the two movements will enjoy a certain amount of inner harmony while also being genuinely versatile and adaptable. They will be an asset when friends and family change priorities; these writers can adapt quickly when changes are made to their schedule.

However, when flexibility is forced upon these people, their rhythm will suffer and while they may experience short periods of happiness. There will be many fluctuations in mood, which they may find difficult to cope with on their own. Talking about their needs and feelings with colleagues, friends, or family will help ease frustration and bring more contentment.

CONNECTED • 4

One of the good things about being a handwriting analyst is having the ability not only to analyze a personality from a handwriting sample, but also to know how best to communicate with people on their own terms. For instance, it is wise to stick to facts and have a logical reason to back up every thought with individuals who join together every letter. But when chatting with disconnected writers, it is a good idea not to ask them to substantiate their ideas with facts because they relate best to feelings, ideas, and hunches, and may well balk.

Factual Person

Sometimes letters can appear to be joined together, but on closer inspection it can be seen that, while the letters are touching each other, they are not actually connected. Look at the "sc" in "scratch." In the word "beware," both the "be" and the "wa" are joined without a connecting stroke. The horizontal mingling indicates that the writer is articulate in expressing everyday facts, but prefers his nearest and dearest to be telepathic about understanding his emotions and when to treat him gently and delicately.

'Twas brillig, and the slithy
gyre and gimbal in the a
All mimsy were the borogrov
momwraths outgabe.
Beware the Jabberwock, my so
that bite and claws that s
the jub-jub bird, and shun
bandersnatch. — Lewis C

feat

Disconnected letters

Disconnected letters

The Scorpio woman has a disconcerting gift that can make icy shivers up your spine. It's a peculiar form of black magic, & she weaves it so expertly, it can seem like real witchcraft. You have very little chance to escape, once your eyes meet hers. Because of her mystical sixth sense, she can often recognize a future mate at first glance, & somehow, she will transfer this perception instantly. You'll have one of two reactions. You'll be hopelessly caught in her spell, & down you'll go, in a dizzy spin towards surrender, or you'll be scared right out of your socks, & feel like running for help. What's the rush?

LINDA GOODMAN'S SUN SIGNS ~ Scorpio

MULTITASKING SAMPLE

...res did
...
...and the
...ith teeth
...h. Beware
...frumious
...oll.

FACTUAL SAMPLE

Letters are touching but are not connected

Multi-Tasking

This is a highly creative and practical person who can think on his feet and find quick solutions to pressing problems. Because this writer has mainly disconnected writing, he is able to undertake many different tasks at the same time. He is able to change his priorities on the spur of the moment should something more important turn up.

Space Between Lines • 1

Video meliora, proboque
Deteriora sequor

How orderly are you?
Handwriting, particularly line spacing, can reveal whether you revel in a daily routine.

The distance between the lines of writing indicates our attitudes toward order. It also shows what importance we attach to having and carrying out a daily routine. If line spacing is balanced, it fits in tastefully with the rest of the space on the paper.

The balance

People who have balanced writing often also have good ideas. They can turn these ideas into a plan of action to achieve a preset goal. Where there is too much space between the lines, the writers tend to have some good ideas, but other creative thoughts they may have are often too dreamlike to be truly workable.

Sometimes writers produce mingling lines. This occurs when the ascenders of the words from one line mix with the descenders of the words from the line above. These are produced by people who have many images and impressions swirling around in their minds. It can be difficult for them to choose where to start and how to make a list of priorities that can be turned into successful action.

How to judge line spacing

This graphic element is one of the more subjective features of assessing someone's writing. It depends to a large extent on how we space our own lines. If we have rather wide spaces between each line, we tend to think that normal line spacing is too close; and, of course, the reverse applies to those who have close spaces between lines.

Normal line spacing is aesthetically pleasing and fits in with the rest of the layout on a page. If you have difficulty determining the spacing between lines, ask a friend who is always full of ideas to write a few lines for you. Find another friend who can sometimes be rather dreamy and utopian and ask them to write a few lines. This will help you to determine what is normal or average spacing between lines.

It is a good idea to look at several samples of writing from the same person; this helps one to gain a true picture of someone's line spacing. When determining line spacing it is best to analyze samples that have been written on paper sized 8½ x 11 inches. This allows writers to choose how much space to put between the lines. Some writers, especially those with large writing, might otherwise have to cramp their writing to fit a small page.

Space Between Lines: The Key

Large spaces between lines indicate an individual who is self-assured, articulate, lucid in thought, far-sighted, orderly, and good at planning. Close spaces indicate an individual who is spontaneous, well-meaning, creative, responsive, impulsive with new ideas, and prone to having short bursts of concentration.

SPACE BETWEEN LINES • 2

Before we start to write, we unconsciously decide how we are going to fill the space on a piece of paper. When we make an accurate judgement, the line spacing will be even and regular throughout the page. When we only have short-term planning skills, we find that when the end of the paper is in sight we still have a lot more to write, so our line spacing becomes narrower to allow all the words to fit on the page.

Spontaneity
This sample's close line spacing plus disconnected letters show that this writer is spontaneous and impulsive and has short bursts of concentration. She also has flashes of intuition and is always ready to introduce more variety into her life.

Horizontal mingling

Disconnected

Competitive golf. is played
mainly on a five and a
half inch course, the space
between your ears.
Bobby Jones.

SPONTANEITY SAMPLE

When you're sad, think about
that would be comforting.
When you're hurt, tell the person
who hurt you. Keeping it inside
makes it grow —

In family life, love is the oil
that eases friction, the cement
that binds closer together, and
the music that brings harmony.

MENTAL AGILITY SAMPLE

Mental Agility

This writer has a dominant lower zone, which makes it difficult to have clear line spacing without leaving huge spaces between the lines. He cleverly leaves sufficient space to make his writing clear and when he writes his lower zones, he either dovetails them (see pages 60–61) with the upper zone on the next line, or he makes the lower zones shorter so that they avoid touching the upper zones on the next line. As this is done unconsciously, it shows his mental agility and speed of thought.

Dovetail

Quick Thinking

This writer gives an excellent example of dovetailing (see pages 60–61). She has chosen to fit the descenders of one line into a space on the next line so

that they do not touch the ascenders. This indicates that the writer is the sort of person who has the ability to think on her feet in difficult situations.

meliora

iota seg

Dovetail

Go play golf. Go to the golf
course. Hit the ball. Find the
ball. Repeat until the ball
is in the hole. Have fun.
The End. = Chuck Hogan.

QUICK THINKING SAMPLE

Space Between Lines • 3

Neque enim quaero
ut credem,

Ideas and dreams
Handwriting gives clues about whether someone turns their ideas into reality or into pleasant dreams.

There are two other factors in line spacing that are also important. One is the distance between the middle zones of each line, and the other is the distance between the descenders in one line and the ascenders in the line below.

The spacing between the lines may appear to be large because there is a great distance between the middle zones in each line. However, where the ascenders and descenders are close —maybe overlapping, but not actually touching—it indicates a clever mind. This feature is called dovetailing and is often found in the writing of gifted, talented, and inventive writers. When the ascenders and descenders touch, hit, or cross each other, this causes the lines to look muddled. It indicates that there are too many ideas floating around in the mind of the writer at any one time and no priorities can be chosen. This may result in a lack of action.

The other aspect of assessing the distance between the lines is to observe the overall use of space between the lines and how it fits in aesthetically with the rest of the space on the paper. When the line spacing becomes too large, these writers tend to allow their ideas to become dreams.

Sometimes you will notice that the distance between the lines varies, with no particular space pattern evident. This can indicate a highly creative individual. It also often means the writer is unconventional and perhaps lacking in inner harmony. The German composer Ludwig van Beethoven (1770–1827) produced very irregular line spacing, and, while we know he was a musical genius with enormous artistic talent, there was also a fair amount of disharmony and unhappiness in his extraordinary life.

Positive application

In brainstorming sessions where lots of ideas are needed, writers with mingling lines are apt to flourish, since they usually have plenty of ideas to offer. Other individuals who perhaps lack creative originality can listen to the stream of ideas and pick out the best workable concepts. An organized plan can then be drawn up and action taken to execute an achievable goal.

People with lots of space between their lines will be able to visualize projects on an overall, grand scale. People with this feature in their writing have the gift of being able to conceptualize something that is new or completely different. However, to be able to make the most of their exciting new ideas and schemes, these people need to be put to work in tandem with other people who are more analytical and practical as well as tactful, logical, firm, and flexible. In this way, the best results for everyone can be achieved quickly and with a sense of positive progress on all sides.

SPACE BETWEEN LINES • 4

It is often said that there is a fine line between genius and serious neurobiological disorders like schizophrenia. The fine-line comparison may also be made with line spacing. Where the ascenders and descenders dovetail, a quick and clever mind is indicated, and someone who can think on their feet with agility and wisdom. When the upper and lower zones touch each other and mingle in the space between the lines, however, the writer will have too many thoughts going around in their head and will not be able to settle on any specific idea or make an instant decision.

Quick Thinker

Although this writer has mainly dominant lower zones, she manages to keep them separate from the upper zones in the next line indicating an ability to think on her feet. She has mainly disconnected letters which show that she enjoys doing a range of tasks at any one time. The rounded letter forms indicate a friendly personality; this conclusion is supported with the warmth of the right slant.

Rounded letter form

In family life, love is the oil that eases friction, the cement that binds closer together, and the music that brings harmony.

General Eva Burrows.

ORGANIZER SAMPLE

Virtually no left margin | Small size

Organizer

This example of clear line spacing indicates clarity of thought, and yet some of the other features in the writing are completely different. This writer has a small absolute size and although she has mainly wide word spacing, she has virtually no left or right margins. This reflects her need to spend time alone. While the past and her family are important to her, the lack of right margin indicates that she enjoys moving forward and acquiring new knowledge.

heu de temps.

sorte de gens:

geances, des

vendeurs

élégantes.

QUICK THINKER SAMPLE

Rounded letter forms

enim
dem,

Word Spacing •1

Nequenenim

Crowded words

*Close word spacing indicates a
person who enjoys being in crowds
and dislikes solitary situations.*

Spacing is one of the few graphic
elements that is found in every
type of written language. The
Roman alphabet, Chinese and
Japanese characters, even Arabic and
Hebrew script all have spacing. It is
one of the vital signs used to analyze
handwriting. For, when you write, you
make an unconscious choice about
how to fill the space.

Imagine that a blank piece of paper
represents the world. The way we fill
that piece of paper shows how we fit
into our environment. The more the ink
trail from the pen fills the paper, the
more we take up space, sometimes
to the extent of intruding into areas
occupied by other people and ignoring
their personal boundaries. The more

spaces there are between the words on
the paper, the more we need to have
time and space to be on our own.

As we go through different stages of
life, our writing changes. When under
great stress, we tend to worry and
become anxious. One of the ways this
may show in our writing is that the
words we write may become more
closely spaced for a while. This inability
to space words normally shows in the
personality of the writer, who finds it
more difficult to organize her life and
also finds it harder to express her
thoughts and needs.

When life returns to normal, the
writer resumes spacing the words the
usual distance from one another and
the personal qualities the writer has
will show once more in her writing.

How to judge word spacing

The lower case "u" is one of the letters
used to establish the space between
words in writing samples. Normal word
spacing occurs when the letter "u" fits
comfortably between each word.

Look at the size the writer has chosen to make their letter "u," and then imagine the "u" sitting comfortably between each word of the writing. This will indicate the writer's normal spacing between words. If there is no room to fit the "u" of the writer between each word, we may say that this indicates close spacing between words. If the letter "u" fits between each word two or more times, this shows that the spacing between words is wide. Word spacing indicates how we fit in with other people, so when we are not completely comfortable with ourselves, we may produce word spacing that is irregular in appearance.

Word Spacing: The Key

Close word spacing indicates an individual who is energetic, bustling, sociable, warm-hearted, chatty, spontaneous, and well-meaning although sometimes too trusting. Wide word spacing indicates an individual who is selective, methodical, reserved, cautious, musical, prioritizes actions, enjoys organizing, prefers one-to-one contact, and makes lists of things to do.

WORD SPACING • 2

Many people write with irregular spacing, with some words close together and other words far apart. Sometimes those who do this will enjoy having company, but at other times they will prefer to relax alone. Introverts tend to recharge their energies while in their own company, while extroverts usually need company to revitalize their drive and motivation. Writers who have a mixture of large and small word spacing are able to relax and make the most of life, whether they are with people or on their own.

Energetic

With close word spacing and a large middle zone, this writer thrives on having lots of company. He is spontaneous, and his use of heavy pressure indicates that he is full of energy and enjoys being with people and socializing. He loves variety in both work and leisure. He likes to live in the present and thinks on his feet when problems arise.

Close word space

"I pulled to the side of the street
book of road maps. But to find
going, you must know where you
didn't. JOHN STEINBECK, P. 966/58

c'est double plaisir
de tromper le trompeur

Jean de la Fontaine

RESERVED SAMPLE

Right slant   Disconnected

Reserved

The wide word spacing means that this writer likes to spend time on his own. The small middle zone in this sample indicates that the writer likes to chat with one person at a time. He uses heavy pressure, disconnected letters, and a slight rightward slant, which show that he is a spontaneous person with lots of ideas that he likes to try out immediately.

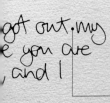

got out. my
e you are
, and I

Close word space

ENERGETIC SAMPLE

Word Spacing • 3

Splendid isolation
Wide word spacing can be one indicator that the writer likes to spend a lot of time on his or her own.

The space between words indicates how people fit into their environment. When words are crowded together, this indicates that it is important for the writer to be surrounded by company. When words are widely spaced, this shows that the writer has a need to spend time alone.

The balance

Balanced word spacing is found where there is clear spacing between the words, and where this spacing fits in aesthetically with the overall layout.

Harmony in word spacing shows that these writers know when to talk and when to listen. They enjoy socializing but they also appreciate time spent on their own. In a working environment, they are usually good teamworkers, fitting in with and adapting to the needs of other members. They tend to be articulate and have self-confidence.

When the space between the words becomes too wide and each word looks like an island in a sea of space, it reveals feelings of isolation. While these writers enjoy spending time on their own, they may want to get along with other people but feel awkward when socializing in a group situation.

When the word spacing is very narrow, these writers feel lonely if left on their own for any length of time. Companionship becomes important since it offers feelings of security.

Positive application

For individuals whose writing shows close spacing, working in a team or in a shared office with several others could be an asset as they feel comfortable among their fellow workers. Good friendships can be forged between two people whose writing exhibits close word spacing. They will both always be ready for a chat and will be delighted to have some company.

People who write with wide spaces between words may prefer to work on their own. Authors could fall into this category. Such people can work in the peace and quiet of their own room and then discuss their task with an editor on a one-to-one basis from time to time, as and when necessary. Very wide word spacing shows someone who is happy with her own company and chooses to socialize spasmodically with a few selected friends. She can surprise others with her wit and repartee in large social gatherings. Such a person appears to enjoy herself, but will be glad when the party is over so that she can return to the peace and quiet of a solitary life. She can put on a mask to cover her true feelings when required to do so.

WORD SPACING • 4

Word spacing is one of the writing movements that emerges from behind the public mask of the writer. It reveals how much individuals enjoy socializing and whether they are comfortable with their own company in solitude. Before you start writing, you do not consciously plan how much space you will leave between each word. You might look at a small piece of paper and reduce the size of your writing if you have a lot to say on it, but your word spacing is an unconscious movement, and one which is virtually impossible to plan. It is this that makes it such a revealing movement.

Spontaneity

This writer has a mixture of close and wide word spacing. There is no pattern as to when the different spacing occurs. His highly disconnected writing indicates that he may enjoy short spells of socializing and brief times alone. The original style indicates that this writer is highly creative and would be excellent in a "think-tank" situation.

Close word space

Wide word space

The years between fifty and seventy
are the hardest. You are always being
asked to do things, and yet you are not
decrepit enough to turn them down.

T. S. Eliot

SPONTANEITY SAMPLE

eue

Sociability

This writer has close word spacing which, coupled with his very connected writing, reflects his love of socializing. His rightward slant shows a warm-hearted personality and the small size of his writing indicates modesty and a thorough approach to the tasks that he undertakes.

Connected letters

> By brooks too broad for keeping
> The lightfoot lads are laid;
> The rose-lipt girls are sleeping
> In fields where roses fade.
>
> 'A Shropshire Lad'
> A.E. Housman.

Righward slant

SOCIABILITY SAMPLE

Dominant middle zone

Upright

> En descendant au salon le
> lendemain matin je me suis
> arrêté un moment au bureau
> de réception de l'hôtel.
> "je suis à court d'argent francais,"
> dis-je à l'employé,

BALANCED SAMPLE

Balanced

At first glance, this writing looks generally balanced, as the spacing between the words and lines makes them look clear, the left margin is fairly straight, and the middle zone is dominant. This writer uses common sense and logic in her approach to life. She is determined to succeed, but she can also empathize with others.

Rhythm • 1

Inopern

Have you got rhythm?
*There is no precise measurement for
assessing rhythm; it depends on the
appraisal of the analyst.*

Rhythm, or the flow of writing,
indicates how much at peace and
in harmony we are within
ourselves. We all have happy and sad
times; we all have change and stress in
our lives at some point. The happier we
are, the more our handwriting rhythm
flows spontaneously. When we are
frustrated, our writing's rhythm may
become tighter or more rigid, and when
we are sad the writing may become
loose and flabby.

Rhythm is one of the graphic
elements that may vary at different
stages of life. However much inner
harmony and balance we may enjoy,
the rhythm of our handwriting will
change when we are going through
a traumatic and difficult time.

Meeting and chatting with people, we
can sometimes manage to put on a
brave face, but inwardly it is not
possible to maintain that control. The
impulses that come from the brain to be
recorded on the paper in the form of
writing will show the real picture of how
the writer is coping with the challenge
of the moment.

The balance

Nobody has perfectly spontaneous and
fluent writing all the time. Some people
will have long spurts of rhythm, which
shows that on the whole they will go
with the flow, enjoy the happy times,
and allow themselves to be sad as
those situations arise.

Others will appear to maintain a
steady rhythm, but closer inspection
reveals a degree of rigidity that affects
the spontaneous flow. These people are
able to be happy within a set
framework: contentment for them means
feeling secure. Following a set
of known and tested rules is the most
important factor in their lives.

How to judge rhythm

Assessing the different types and degrees of rhythm in handwriting is more a question of artistic appraisal than of following fixed guidelines.

Rhythm is created by the spontaneous movements in writing. Imagine a glider in the clear, blue sky on a lovely sunny day. Visualize the graceful turns made to fit in with the changing air stream and varying direction. The whole forms a peaceful scene with flowing, yet also irregular changes. If a sudden air current appears, the glider will experience some turbulence; the calm scene will become jerky until the air flow is restored and once more the regular, elegant movements of the glider can be observed.

Rhythm: The Key

Rhythmic writing indicates an individual who is musical, sensible, patient, tolerant, calm, and consistent. Arrhythmic writing indicates an individual who is sensitive, artistic, excitable, has lots of interests, and is perhaps an inventor, or has the talent of a genius.

RHYTHM · 2

Sometimes people want to change aspects of their character—perhaps to gain contentment, or to learn more confidence; there are many possible reasons. These individuals may be prescribed a daily writing exercise by a graphotherapist. One of the ways in which their progress can be monitored is by observing the changes in rhythm that will be displayed in their ordinary writing. The rhythmic flow of their handwriting will gradually become more spontaneous, and this will affect their character as the changes become absorbed by their unconscious so that positive personality transformation can emerge.

Rounded (indicating kindness)

Angle (indicating firmness)

What kind of noise annoys
an oyster? A noisy noise
annoys an oyster -

KNOWING GOALS SAMPLE

Knowing Goals

This writer demonstrates a fairly flowing rhythm. This shows that she knows what she wants in life and is content with the choices she makes. She can be kind but is also firm, with the ability to look after herself in a way that brings harmony to her inner self. The rightward slant and garland letter forms show that she has a friendly, empathetic personality.

In The generality of men are naturally apt to be swayed by fear rather than reverence, and to refrain from evil rather because of the punishment that it brings than because of its own foulness. Aristotle

Narrow width

Broad width

DISCIPLINED SAMPLE

Disciplined Approach

Looking at this sample of rhythm, we can see that the writer finds harmony through a more disciplined approach to life. This writer deals with life with a certain sensitive precision, which makes her feel secure.

Wavy line

Oui, Ah, j'y pense. Il me faut des cigarettes. Voulez-vous avoir le bonté de me dire s'il y a un bureau de tabac près ici?

CREATIVITY SAMPLE

Creativity

In this sample, the writing is irregular in every way, which means it is difficult to observe any rhythm in it. This writer is creative, full of ideas, and intuitive; her wide word spacing indicates that she prefers to mix on a one-to-one basis rather than in large crowds.

Rhythm • 3

A graphic element
Graphologists need to observe correctly and to develop the ability to appraise rhythm from an artistic viewpoint.

Rhythm is one of the graphic elements that is completely unique to each of us. Rhythm is a true sign of the state of the innermost self, and of the degree of calm acceptance the writer is able to bring to facing life at that time.

We should check whether the rhythm in someone's writing is free flowing and spontaneous. If it is disturbed we look to see whether the disturbance occurs over long or short stretches.

Rhythm is certainly not easy to observe correctly. However, when trying to identify a fairly flowing rhythm, it may

help you to imagine the swinging of a hammock. Its swings are not always consistent, but they do recur intermittently, and with a certain dependability. If you apply this image to the rhythm in the writing, it is easier to imagine how such writers bring a degree of method and an individual harmony to their lives.

Look also at the rigidity of someone's rhythm. It may help to imagine the keys on a piano. The black keys appear with absolute regularity in sets of two, then there is a space, and then three black keys; this forms a fixed and repetitive pattern. If this image can be applied to a piece of writing, you are looking at a rigid rhythm. It does show rhythmic changes, but they occur at fixed intervals with no variation.

This rigidity reflects the methods such writers use to find protection, safety, and refuge—by keeping a rigid discipline in daily living—but it also indicates that they will experience fear if their usual pattern is broken for some reason. Their unconscious response will take the form of either fight or flight, depending on what other indications are present in the writing.

Positive application

A degree of rigidity in writing shows individuals who are generally balanced in their approach to life and can be flexible when the situation demands a change of priorities and actions. They exert a stable influence in group situations.

When a writing style has no evidence of a flow, it is often because the writer has a wealth of ideas, and is able to work on lots of different projects at any one time. Short spurts of spontaneous, flowing rhythm can give some people moments of ecstasy while writing, but those who write with stilted rhythm generally prefer stable periods of contentment rather than spasms of euphoria. Happiness for one person may be purgatory for another—observe the difference between those who enjoy dangerous sports and those who just enjoy watching dangerous sports!

RHYTHM • 4 One of the

reasons why rhythm is so exciting is because it reveals different aspects of rigidity. Nineteenth-century writing displays a stiff, rigid rhythm. Contemporary writing shows a different sort of rigidity: for instance, rigidity within the broad italic style, or a rigidly narrow, angular style. There is much more roundness and flexibility in the rhythm. This shows that while today's writers like to have rules, they are also willing to be flexible and see another point of view.

Connectedness

Logical

The rhythmic flow of this writer is assisted by the connectedness and the garland letter forms of the handwriting. This person will deal with other people in a logical and friendly way.

LOGICAL SAMPLE

Easygoing

This writer has an easy, flowing rhythm with a slight rightward slant in their writing, which shows that they have healthy emotional responses and an ability to take life as it comes. The balanced zones and slightly broad width convey that they have an open-minded approach to unfamiliar situations.

Hold on

The way you hold your pen will affect the style of your writing.

Inopem me copsia fecit

EASYGOING SAMPLE

Slightly broad width

Regularity •1

Creativity or self-discipline?
The degree of regularity displayed in a writing style will indicate the person's degree of creativity.

Regularity in writing indicates our approach to work and also shows how we achieve contentment. Regular writing indicates that the writer appreciates being shown what to do and knowing the boundaries. When the writing is irregular, the writer prefers to perform tasks in his own way.

Regularity is just one indicator that shows we cannot copy a writing style exactly; we all reveal our own little idiosyncrasies through our writing. There are so many places where irregularities can be found in handwriting that this movement is a great asset in finding characteristics that apply solely to an individual writer. It doesn't matter whether the script is Chinese or Hebrew, Japanese or Russian, French or German—every single person writes using some sort of small variation from the copybook that was followed in school. That is what makes every human being so wonderfully unique. While we may have some ability to learn to be more disciplined or creative, we will always retain a preference for different kinds of boundaries.

The balance

Sometimes we look at a piece of writing and cannot tell whether it is regular or not. When this happens, it generally means that the writer is well-balanced and knows when to use and apply self-discipline and when to allow creativity to flow. It indicates a generally spontaneous person who can curb their liveliness when required.

When writing is very regular, it shows an individual who is keen to know and follow a given set of rules. When writing appears to have no order on a page and looks very irregular, the writer is spontaneous and possibly highly creative, but will have difficulty conforming to rules and regulations.

How to judge regularity

Visualize a row of soldiers on the parade ground. Transfer this imagined picture to the sample of writing you are analyzing; if the letters appear like soldiers then the writing is regular. When a sample of writing does not fit this picture, the script is probably irregular. For the serious student, there is a set of measurements that may be followed. However, in the first instance, it is wise to learn to look at an entire sample of writing and observe the amount of regularity that is present at first glance. Another aid is to look at some of the other movements that are present—consider whether the pressure is evenly distributed over the whole sample, or whether letter forms are consistent throughout.

Regularity: The Key

Regular writing indicates an individual who is balanced, disciplined, methodical, orderly, single-minded, and has willpower and self-control. Irregular writing indicates someone who is spontaneous, creative, impulsive, enjoys variety, and has emotional warmth.

REGULARITY • 2

Sometimes people wonder if there is a perfect way to write, but the truth is that there is no ideal handwriting. Let us take regularity as an example. People who are highly creative will have irregular writing; these uneven movements show that original thoughts and concepts flourish in the mind of the writer. On the other hand, where exactness, precision, and routine are required for a task, it will be essential to ensure that the person undertaking it has regular handwriting.

Variety

The irregular writing in this sample shows that the writer enjoys lots of variety in all parts of her life. She looks forward to new and unknown ventures. The heavy pressure she uses indicates that she has plenty of energy and can become so involved with what she is doing that she can lose all track of time.

First irregular letter form "n"

Irregular letter form

ama

We praise a man who feels
angry on the right grounds and
against the right persons and
also in the right manner at
the right moment and for
the right length of time.
What is a friend?
A single soul dwelling in
two bodies
Aristotle

Long starting stroke

Narrow width

ROUTINE SAMPLE

Long end stroke

Second irregular letter form "n"

la matinée?
Je me suis
amps - Elysées.

VARIETY SAMPLE

Routine

This is a good example of regularity, because there are many features which are similar. The writer likes routine, and her long starting strokes show that she likes to prepare herself for special occasions. A complementary feature of the writing is its narrowness, which indicates that she likes to follow known rules.

Regularity • 3

Regular or irregular?
Whatever the degree of irregularity revealed in your writing, you could be highly successful.

It is interesting to note that very successful people may have either highly regular or extremely irregular writing. Every individual may have the qualities that are needed to fulfill their goals, despite being at different ends of the spectrum in this area.

A genius may have handwriting that is totally illegible and possibly even looks a mess on the page. The enormous amount of irregularity created by the writer shows that originality comes from within and the form it takes is unique to that individual. People whose jobs require them to exercise a great deal of self-discipline may have exceedingly regular writing. They may excel at sports or perhaps work in an area of industry where exactness and precision are required.

As the amount of regularity that shows in handwriting comes from the core of someone's personality, it is a very useful way of getting behind the mask of an individual. Many people think that monks who lived in religious orders centuries ago were very disciplined. However, if you ever have the opportunity to visit a monastery or a museum, look at some of the books that were written in the calligraphic style by those monks. You will notice that, although the overall look of the writing on the page may be regular, there will be little irregularities which will have been made by each different monk who worked on the document. The more irregularities that appear in the writing on the manuscript, the more creative—and possibly averse to following discipline—was the monk.

Positive application

People with regular writing enjoy method and order in life. Following an established, structured system makes them feel secure. They also have a sense of duty and are usually dependable and reliable about completing tasks on time. The more regular the writing, the longer the concentration span. This can be helpful to people who have to perform certain tasks within set time limits. They are usually industrious and will persevere until a solution is found or a job completed.

People with irregular writing show their emotions and tend to enjoy a variety of interests. They are often creative and have unaffected, natural personalities. Slightly irregular writing with firm pressure, half-connectedness, a mixture of letter forms, some broad strokes, and medium spurts of spontaneous rhythm, will indicate someone who is friendly, flexible, versatile, energetic, and practical— a great combination of traits.

REGULARITY • 4

Those who have irregular writing may work well with people who have regular writing. Individuals with irregular writing will have creative inspiration, while those with regular writing will be able to carry out all the necessary thorough trials and tests required to see whether a project is viable. When these two different types of people work together, they can make an excellent team and produce outstanding results. Irregular writing is easier to analyze because the unique qualities of such writers stand out. The analyst sometimes has to look carefully at regular writing because its unique traits are often well hidden.

Straight left margin

Even spacing

One passes through the wo
if any, of the important t
the people with whom one
the closest intimacy.

ama

Variety

This writer has irregular writing, which indicates that she enjoys doing lots of different things. Look at the different sizes in the middle zone, showing her versatility and willingness to try anything new. The slightly leftward slant shows that her family are important to her. It also suggests that she likes to make new decisions based on past experiences.

When you're sad think about what would be comforting. When you're hurt, tell the person who hurt you. Keeping it inside makes it grow.

Unknown.

VARIETY SAMPLE

Irregular letter form

Differently sized middle zones

Same letter forms

knowing few,

gs about even

as been .... in

ROUTINE SAMPLE

Routine

This writing is a good example of regularity. The slant, size, spacing, and letter forms are all written in a regular pattern. This writer enjoys working to a known routine and prefers to work on one task at a time. When he has completed this task, he is ready to move on to the next assignment. With his straight left margin, he exercises self-discipline in order to achieve his goals in the time he has allowed himself through careful planning.

Style •1

Dramatic or balanced?
*Our handwriting style can reveal
whether we have an artistic or
a scientific tendency.*

At school we were taught to write
in a certain way. As fashions
change, so do copybooks,
and styles vary from time to time. As we
grow up, the style of our writing often
changes and this is reflected in how
we are influenced by both people and
experiences. The new way in which we
write represents the different priorities
and behavior patterns we wish to adopt
in our lives.

The balance

What is a balanced style to one person
may not be balanced to another. Some
people like to see loops in handwriting,
while others hate any extra flourishes

that are made to the essential stroke.
The French and the Italians tend to
be dramatic and to have expressive
personalities; this is reflected in the
loops and flourishes of their copybook.
Until the Second World War, the British
copybook was made up of letters with
completed loops. Shortly after the war,
the copybook changed and children
were taught to write with straight strokes
at the top and unfinished loops at the
bottom of some letters.

How to judge style

To assess style, it is necessary to be
aware of the copybook from which the
writer was taught. When you know this,
look at the writing and decide whether
more strokes have been added to the
copybook style, or whether there are
fewer strokes apparent on the page.

If the copybook style of the writer is
unknown, you need to decide which
strokes are absolutely essential to the
legibility of the writing. Next, observe
whether additions to or subtractions
from these strokes can actually be seen

in the writing. Try to assess whether the ultimate legibility of the writing has been affected by these strokes.

A simplified writing style contains the essential strokes, while an enriched writing may contain extra strokes such as loops. A neglected style will be missing some essential lines, which may affect legibility. When there is a lot of rigidity in the writing, this may indicate that the writer has a style very near that of the copybook followed at school.

People with an enriched writing style may have difficulty recognizing a neglected style, and vice versa. If you are not sure about your own writing, try comparing it with samples from people whom you know to be extravagant, and samples from people who live simply.

Style: The Key

An enriched style indicates an individual who has a flair for design, for whom rich colors are important. It may also show someone's liking for ornaments and pictures. A simplified style indicates an individual with an objective, scientific, and matter-of-fact approach—someone interested only in essential facts.

STYLE · 2

When learning to understand the implications of style, it can be helpful to look at the handwriting of people you know. Ask someone who loves bright colors and adornments in their home to write you a sample, and then ask someone who keeps chat to a minimum and likes to find practical solutions speedily when problems arise. Note the differences in their writing. The colorful personality with enriched style will have a lot of extra strokes, while the person who sticks to the essentials will have the minimum strokes required to form each letter. This writing style will be simplified.

Plenty of Ideas

The loops in the upper zone of this handwriting indicate that this writer has plenty of ideas. There are some letters that are connected together, showing that she has a gift that allows her to look at intuitive ideas logically and to choose which are viable and can be converted into realistic goals.

Upper zone loop

Upper zone loop

More important than talent, strength or knowledge is the ability to laugh at yourself and enjoy the pursuit of your dreams.

Amy grant

IDEAS SAMPLE

medio

Practical Approach

This simplified writing style is that of a person with a practical approach to life and plenty of common sense. Many of her letters are not joined to each other, which means she is able to handle several tasks at one time. Her left margin becomes gradually larger, as the space to the left of the page increases with each line that has been written. This shows that, when she meets people, she may be cautious at first, but once she gets to know them, she will enjoy their friendship.

Increasing
left margin

Here dead we lie because we did not choose
To live and shame the land from which we sprung.
Life, to be sure, is nothing much to lose;
But young men think it is, and we were young.

PRACTICAL SAMPLE

Disconnection

Mental Energy

This writer has loops which can be seen in both the ascenders and descenders. She also has very connected writing and uses light pressure. This indicates that she uses a lot of mental energy and may enjoy reminiscing about her past. The right slant indicates that she is quite a romantic at heart.

Lower
zone loops

Love and putting are mysteries for
the philosopher to solve. Both
subjects are beyond golfers.

ENERGY SAMPLE

Style • 3

Style and fashion
*Extra loops and twirls in someone's
writing denote a flamboyant, possibly
unconventional, character.*

Some people are very aware of style or wear flamboyant clothes. These individuals may enhance their writing style with additions to the fundamental writing movements. The more unconventional their appearance, the more likely their handwriting is to have an enriched style, with loops and extra twirls attached to the letters.

Positive application

People who work in the fashion industry may have very flamboyant writing. They may have their own individual ideas on how to make the best use of different fabrics, and what sorts of accessories will blend in well with them. Their overall appearance has a recognizable, personalized style and this is reflected in their writing style.

At the opposite end of the spectrum are individuals who choose to write using only basic strokes to ensure legibility and nothing more. They tend to be objective and analytical, and to concentrate on facts. They work speedily and can usually think on their feet. Clarity of thought, articulate delivery, and simplicity as a way of life are often characteristics of these writers.

It is very difficult to maintain the exact copybook style learnt at school, and convention tends to play an important role in the lives of those who continue to write as they were taught. For them, happiness, security, and contentment are obtained by following rules.

In some schools, the calligraphic style is taught. While uniformity of size and width of letters are important, it is fascinating to note that, in a class of students who have had the same teacher, each student will write calligraphy in a slightly different style.

Neglected writing style happens when strokes that are essential to legibility are missing. This writing needs careful attention. An experienced analyst will be able to deduce the reason for this particular type of writing. Sometimes neglected style occurs because someone's thoughts rush out in such a hurry that the person's hand cannot keep up with their brain.

Remember to consider the significance of the pen that someone is using to write with. The thicker the pen stroke, the more likely it is that the writer will be a stylish dresser; thin pen strokes often signify people who prefer the simple things in life.

Style: The Key

Copybook style indicates an individual who is good at following rules, reliable, and enjoys working in teams. Neglected style denotes an individual who thinks quickly and comes up with lots of ideas.

STYLE • 4

Some copybook styles are easier to recognize than others. The Palmer method, as taught in many American schools, does stand out with its distinct right slant, flowing connected letters, and fully formed upper and lower loops. Whatever the alphabet, from a roman calligraphic style to Chinese characters, every writer will bring their own unique touches to the style they have been taught. It is interesting to observe the individual strokes that make up each Chinese character. These strokes may be longer, more curved, and even made with a thicker or thinner stroke than the original copybook method prescribed.

Aspirational

This writer has enriched loops in the upper and lower zones, indicating that his ideas are both skillfully creative as well as aspirational. The dominant lower zone with some large enriched loops indicates a desire for security. There are also some straight downstrokes in the lower zone, which reflect his ability to be practical and complete a task speedily when time becomes a priority. His spontaneous and irregular style shows his flexibility, and his ability to change priorities.

Enriched loop

Happily Creative

A naturally creative and genuine person is shown by the irregularity and spontaneity in this handwriting. It contains just a few enhancements. The loops in both the upper and lower zones indicate that she is able to turn ideas into reality, and that she can attain her goals and reach successful conclusions. Some rhythm shows in the writing. This, with the originality shown by the middle zone, ensures that this lady will make the most of the happy times she experiences in life.

The problems of victory are more agreeable than the problems of defeat, but they are no less difficult.

Winston Churchill

HAPPILY CREATIVE SAMPLE

Upper zone loop

Lower zone loop

ASPIRATIONAL SAMPLE

Enriched loop

Downstroke without loop

Baselines • 1

I am seques

A stable baseline
*This can indicate common sense,
while a wavy baseline may indicate that
the writer has some emotional problems.*

The baseline is the path that we make as we write across the page. This imaginary line indicates our mood of the moment. When we are happy, the baseline may rise slightly and when we are tired or sad, the words may dip toward the end of the line.

The balance

A usually stable baseline that more or less sticks to the path shows that, while we have the discipline to maintain stability, we are also able to allow our emotions to be released as and when necessary. Slightly rising or falling baselines may indicate our feelings of the moment. When we are excited, happy, or looking forward to the future, we often produce a baseline that rises.

When we are faced with adversity—for instance, when we have to work a lot of overtime, or are just exhausted—then the baseline is inclined to fall.

The baseline tells us how we are feeling at the time we are writing, so it is helpful to look at other handwriting movements to ensure that we are making correct interpretations. The more a baseline rises or falls, the more strongly an emotion is felt and sometimes displayed.

How to assess baselines

If the baseline is not immediately visible to the eye, take a ruler and place it at the base of a writing line. This may help you to follow the writing path across the page. Alternatively, turn the paper over so that you are looking at the blank side. Now look through the paper and see if a pattern emerges for the baseline.

When individuals are going through a turbulent time and their emotions are upset, then their writing may show a variety of baselines, with some rising, and others falling. This creates a baseline that runs across the page in a generally wavy, undulating manner.

There are a couple of unusual baselines which may not appear on first inspection. A concave baseline can be seen when there is a slight dip in the middle of the line before the words rise again toward the end of the line (imagine a washing line strung up in such a way that both ends are higher than the middle). The opposite of a concave baseline is a convex baseline.

Baselines: The Key

A rising baseline indicates an individual who is happy, optimistic, and can rise to a challenge. A falling one shows someone who is exhausted, overworked, and stressed. A stable baseline suggests a person who is practical, self-disciplined, keeps calm in a crisis, and has plenty of common sense. A wavy baseline means that the writer is emotional, imaginative, creative, and full of ideas. A concave baseline indicates an individual who is reliable, thorough, and will complete tasks. A convex baseline reveals a person who is good at getting projects started, with plenty of short-term enthusiasm.

BASELINES • 2

When we write, we are totally unaware of the path the pen makes across the page to create the baseline. It is only when a piece of paper is full of writing and we look at the end result that we can see the pattern of the baselines. While this feature of handwriting is unique to every writer, it is also one of the writing movements we make that will change from time to time. However, it is important to note that writers will be unconscious of any changes to their baselines, since how they manifest always depends on writers' feelings at the time they are writing. Thus, baselines may be more revealing than movements, which can be disguised.

Thorough Approach

Look at the way the baseline dips steeply in the middle of this sample; it is rather like a hammock. There is no left margin and very little right margin. This writer may take some time to become enthusiastic about trying out new ideas and launching into tasks, but once she sets her mind on finding out what is going on, she will end up giving all of her energy to doing a thorough job and achieving a goal.

End of concave baseline

Start of concave baseline

> Hazel had picked a fresh bay-leaf from a tree by the river and he had dropped it in.

THOROUGH APPROACH SAMPLE

Human Approach

This stable baseline has been produced by someone who is warm-hearted, modest, and has a very human, commonsense approach to life. She knows when to be empathetic and when to be disciplined. The thick stroke of the pen and the small size of her writing show a gentle and discreet nature.

Change doesn't cause pain: resistance to change is what causes pain.

Anonymous.

Stable baseline

HUMAN APPROACH SAMPLE

Sociable

The rising baseline and large middle zone show that this writer is fun, sociable, and keen to try out new and exciting ventures. She will be a positive team member and able to fit in with different circumstances as they arise.

Always laugh if you can, it is a cheap medicine; merriment is a philosophy not well understood. It is the sunny side of existence. Byron.

Rising baseline

SOCIABLE SAMPLE

Baselines • 3

Rising and falling
When writing early in the day, you are likely to produce a rising baseline but later, the baseline is apt to drop.

A sample for analysis should be written on plain paper so that the analyst can establish the writer's general mood. Some people say they always write on lined paper. They may find writing on lines encourages self-discipline and keeps them more stable.

If you look at samples of writing written by the same person at different stages in their life, you may notice that the baseline changes in the various samples according to their mood. Thus, it is helpful to look at several samples.

Positive application

Writers with rising baselines are usually positive, extrovert, and lively. They enjoy adventure, new challenges, and often have a pioneering spirit.

A baseline that runs more or less straight along the page shows stability, self-discipline, and a feeling of being in control. Baselines fall when a person goes through periods of overwork, overstress, and exhaustion. If you write in the morning, you may notice that the baselines rise and if you write again in the evening after an exhausting day, you will often find that the baseline is now falling. After a good night's sleep or a vacation, the writing line will return to normal again.

When people write in wavy lines across the page, they usually wear their hearts on their sleeves. They have strong emotions and they like others to know when they are ecstatically happy as well as when they are in the depths of despair. These people can be great fun to be around when they feel that life is treating them well.

Baselines that sink in the middle of a line are produced by writers who are reliable and thorough. If they are taking part in a project, they may show little enthusiasm at first but grow increasingly involved as the project unfolds. Their enthusiasm develops over time and they will finish strongly, having seen the job through to its conclusion.

Baselines that rise in the middle of a line are called convex baselines. They are created by writers who can influence a team of people with their enthusiasm. They can inject a rush of adrenaline into a project and provide a buzz of enthusiasm that gets a project off the ground. They prefer short projects, because it is difficult for them to remain devoted to one project over a long period of time.

The baseline is one of the few handwriting movements where it is more balanced to have one sort rather than a mixture of different types. For instance, if someone can maintain a slightly rising baseline, it shows that they will also be able to maintain a positive outlook.

BASELINES • 4

A slightly rising baseline shows optimism, and when heavy pressure is also found in the writing, it indicates that someone has the energy as well as the right attitude to reach the goals they are set. When a baseline rises steeply and the pressure becomes either irregular or light, it means that the writer is putting on a brave face in adverse circumstances. For example, someone may have an illness that prevents them from leading a full life, but they are still keen to put what energy they have available to positive and profitable use.

Rising line begins

Positive Approach

This writer with rising baselines is positive, adventurous, kind, and warm-hearted. The irregularity in her handwriting movements and the mixture of letter forms show that she can look at ideas from many different angles. She has a good eye for detail, when it is required, and an excellent sense of humor.

Voici votre b
monsieur, il v
cent vingt-tr
En quelle da
vous?

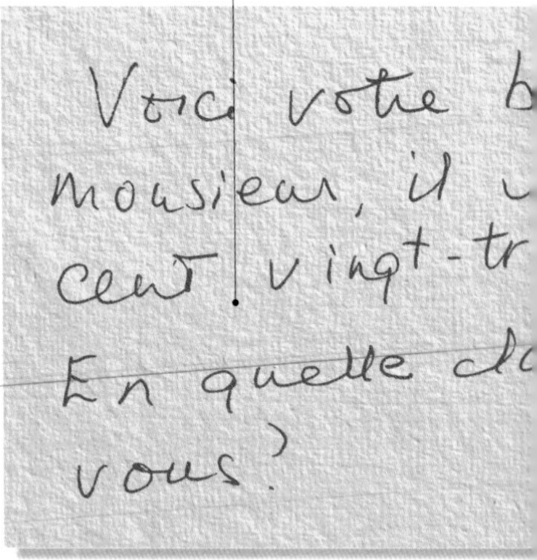

Up and down the City
Road, in and out the
eagle. Thats the way
the money goes. Pop
goes the weasel.
W. R. Mandale.

Concave baseline ends

Concave baseline begins

TIRED SAMPLE

letin

cing

à payer

e voyager.

Tired

At first glance, this writing looks as though it has fairly straight baselines. However, when you measure it with a ruler, you will see that the first three lines are falling and the next two are concave. What is also interesting is that the last letter on the line sometimes rises. This shows a writer who is tired at the time of writing, but who normally has a positive and optimistic outlook on life.

Garland letter form

POSITIVE APPROACH SAMPLE

Pressure • 1

Heavy or light?
The pressure used can indicate levels of energy, both physical and mental, that the writer has.

Pressure is the mark we make on the paper, and it tells us all about how much energy we have and how we use it. The more energy we have available, the heavier the indentation we leave behind on the paper. No matter what script or language is used, whether the writing is from left to right, right to left, or vertically inscribed, when the pen touches the paper, it leaves an indent. To the naked eye, it may not be visible, but the expert analyst, with the aid of a magnifying glass, will be able to detect pressure from a mark.

The balance

When people wrote with quill pens, it was easy to see if they wrote in balance. There would be a heavier, slightly darker downstroke, and a lighter, slightly thinner upstroke. Individuals who wrote with this balance would use their energy wisely. They would work hard and then enjoy their well-earned relaxation time. They would leave sufficient time to sleep so that their energy could be restored.

While heavy pressure shows lots of energy, if it becomes too heavy, it may be an indication of overstress. If the pressure is on the light side, choices must be made about how to use the energy that is available. Some individuals may enjoy physical activities, while others prefer to use their energy in a mental capacity. Those with lighter pressure tend to tire more easily and need more sleep to feel completely refreshed. Even when we are healthy, we have different levels of energy available. Genuine acceptance can help us to use our vitality wisely.

How to judge pressure

The best way to recognize pressure is to compare someone you know who is always bounding with energy with someone who is easily tired. Ask them both to write a few lines for you. Now, put your fingers on the reverse side of the paper on which they have written. Gently feel the indentation marks. The person with heavy marks will have left plenty of evidence. The individual who becomes easily tired may not appear to have left any indentation in the paper.

Finally, write a few lines yourself and compare your own pressure with the two samples. You will then have an idea as to how much pressure you exert. You may also find it interesting to talk to the other two people and see whether they have any observations.

Pressure: The Key

Heavy pressure indicates an individual with energy, vitality, determination, and strength. Light pressure indicates an individual who is flexible, adaptable, sensitive, tender, but has only short bursts of concentration.

PRESSURE · 2

When writing a sample for analysis, it is important to place the piece of paper on a pad of paper or a magazine to ensure that the true pressure can be seen. If the paper rests on a wooden desk, then the grains from the wood will give a false picture of the pressure applied. Similarly, hard surfaces such as kitchen worktops will also prevent the true pressure from showing. Writing a sample in a moving vehicle is also to be avoided, because this will make handwriting movements jerky.

Determined

This lady writes with irregular pressure, which shows that when she is interested in something, she will give all of her energy to the project in hand until it is finished, and only then will she rest. Movements that support this interpretation are the narrowness of the width and the rigidity of the rhythm in the handwriting. The pressure is irregular, meaning she will sometimes overexert herself in the enthusiasm of the moment. Then she will need a while to recuperate her vitality. The fine pen stroke shows her sensitive nature. She will often put on a brave face when hurt and may use wit to disguise her feelings.

Connected letter

[Handwritten sample - Energy and Creativity]

Running water Never disappointed
Crossing water always. Something
Stepping stones were stations of the soul,

A kesh could mean the track of some
carrying a convey
raised above the waters of a bog
Or the convey where it bridged old

drains + streams

It steadies me to tell these things Also
I cannot mention keshes or the ford
without my father. Sha she appearing to me

On a path towards sunset, eyeing spades
and clothes
That turf cutters showed perhaps
or some cart off
Before they crossed the log that off
spans the burn

Poem by SEAMUS HEANEY from
"Opened ground"

ENERGY AND CREATIVITY SAMPLE

Creative style

Rigid rhythm   Narrow width

[Handwritten sample - Determined]

he service clause
who confers it.

DETERMINED SAMPLE

Energy and Creativity

This sample has been written using heavy pressure. The writer puts a lot of energy into her life, especially through her creativity. She has some wonderfully original ideas and can get carried away with her enthusiasm, not realizing that, despite having plenty of energy, she can also get tired. The sharpness and originality in this writing show a sensitive person who is versatile and has many interests.

Pressure • 3

Measure your energy
Handwriting with heavy pressure suggests lots of stamina and a love of the outdoor life.

Many people associate pressure in handwriting with physical energy. While this is certainly the case, the extent of handwriting pressure also indicates our mental and emotional energies—the stamina we have to keep going, and the energy we have to fight until we see justice in action. Sometimes people write with irregular pressure. There will be some heavy bursts intermingled with light pressure. The experienced analyst is trained to interpret what is happening to the energy as a whole.

Some people like to start the day gently and gradually increase their speed until they are using all their energies. Their writing shows a lighter pressure at the top of the long stroke in a letter such as an "h" and a heavier pressure at the lower end. This is an indication that they take time to get themselves moving.

Whatever pressure you write with, you will notice that it changes after you exercise. It will become irregular for perhaps half an hour after you stop being active. It is quite difficult to write in your normal style after exercise, since you do not have the control over your body that you usually have.

Positive application

Individuals who write using firm pressure tend to have self-discipline: they can see a task through to completion, whatever its complexity and challenges. They have an inner determination to keep going whatever the circumstances. They also tend to enjoy physical sports, pursue outdoor adventures, or take part in pioneering expeditions. Individuals who write using heavy pressure are often bounding with energy and appear to need very little sleep.

People who write with light pressure are good at ordering their priorities and being flexible. They have the ability to change their direction and adapt to new situations speedily. Generally mentally agile and receptive to new ideas, they prefer to discuss rather than argue; peace and calm are important to them. They are often analytical thinkers with sharp minds that penetrate to the core of a problem in order to find solutions.

Writers with lighter pressure may well be drawn to pursuits such as tai chi and forms of yoga for which little physical energy is needed. Those whose writing displays medium pressure will know how to balance their energy output, giving time to mental pursuits as well as physical activities. They know that if they have to overexert themselves on occasion, whether for work or pleasure, they can always replenish their energy levels with an early night.

PRESSURE • 4

Pressure indicates the energy available and how it is being used; for example, we can be physically active and yet mentally or emotionally exhausted. The pressure may become irregular or light while we are going through a difficult or challenging phase. It is one thing to put all one's vitality into one aspect of one's life; it is quite another matter to be able to balance the energy output equally across all areas. In times of stress, we put our strength into dealing with the immediate challenge. As we become used to new circumstances, our energy output may become more balanced.

Slow Starter

This person's handwriting demonstrates the uniqueness of pressure very well. Look carefully at the end of one of the descenders, such as an "f." You may have to use a magnifying glass to see clearly. You will notice that the color of the ink is slightly darker toward the end, showing that the writer uses more pressure at the end of the stroke. This individual may be slow to get going, but once she starts work, she will gradually find that she has more energy available as the day goes on. If you look at descenders such as the lower case "g" you will see that these strokes end in a fine point and the ink shade is lighter. This shows that she has great sensitivity.

Descender ending with increased pressure

Descender ending in sharp point

" Yes, I am a dreamer. For find his way by moonlight, the rest of the world. "

Conflict

The irregular and mainly light pressure used in this sample may be caused by the rightward slant and the slightly falling baselines. This writer has a lot of drive, but tires easily, causing her frustration. The slight rise in the middle of the baseline shows a moment in which she is hoping that enthusiasm will make up for her lack of vitality. This person is friendly, and also determined. You can see this by the mixture of angle and garland letter forms contained in the script. Although the writing may look fairly regular, this is a mask. Look at the two "p"s in the word "happen"; they are two very different sizes.

Many are called, but few are chosen. Trouble is what happen when you are not called, but find yourself chosen?

CONFLICT SAMPLE

Large middle zone   Small middle zone

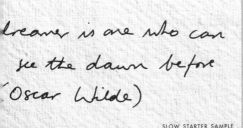

dreamer is one who can see the dawn before (Oscar Wilde)

SLOW STARTER SAMPLE

Pen Stroke •1

novatrix

Pasty or sharp?
A thick pen stroke is known as "pasty," while a thin stroke is called "sharp."

The width of the stroke that the pen leaves on the paper tells us something about the material and spiritual aspirations of the writer. For example, while many people enjoy beauty in one form or another, the writer with the thicker stroke will feel beauty sensually, while the writer who prefers to produce a thinner stroke will feel the beauty mentally. However, one has to be careful to ascertain whether the writer had any choice in the pen used for the sample before making any assumptions about their character.

The balance

An appreciation of beauty is personal to each of us, so there will be some margin as to what constitutes balance.

The use of a pen stroke of medium-thickness indicates that we enjoy socializing and the good life. We will also derive pleasure from working hard and giving our attention to producing a thorough job well done. We know when to sacrifice quality for common sense and when to push for the best that life has to offer us. There is also a healthy balance between enjoying material possessions and heeding moral values and ethics.

Where the pen stroke is slightly thicker, it is called a pasty stroke. The writer probably has an easygoing nature and a broad-minded outlook. Such a person may be full of ideas, but prefers to delegate the details of action to others. Someone who tends to write with a thinner pen stroke is more inclined to be analytical, and will have a sharp, penetrating brain. For this kind of person, finding the root cause of a problem may bring satisfaction. When simplification is also present in such writing, the writer will find a quick and long-lasting solution to any problem.

How to judge thickness

In today's world, where we often pick up the nearest pen in order to write, this particular aspect of handwriting can be difficult to evaluate correctly. Look at the thickness of the writing and see how it appears to you. If you are not sure, look at the tip of the stroke at the end of a word and observe whether it ends in a point. If it does, then you are probably looking at a sharp, or thin, pen stroke. An expert analyst would look at the stroke under a magnifying glass to enable them to determine the stroke pattern.

If you are in doubt about a pen stroke, leave it out of your analysis. It can be difficult to tell how much it has been influenced by the choice of pen.

Pressure: The Key

Pasty writing or writing with thick strokes indicates an individual who is broad-minded, easygoing, colorful, vital, and to whom the senses are important. Sharp or thin writing indicates an individual who is refined, sensitive, ethical, and analytical.

PEN STROKE • 2

Ask ten different people to use the same pen to produce their writing sample. If you had not watched these individuals using the same pen, you would think that several different pens had been used. Those who like to make a thick stroke on the page will hold the pen in such a way that the ink trail comes out with the widest possible path. Those who like the look of a thin pen stroke will hold the pen in a different way to give a fine appearance to the ink trail on the paper.

Analytical

This sample's fine, sharp stroke reflects the analytical mind of the writer. Its dominant lower zone indicates that she likes to delve into and discover how things work and what makes people tick. The upright slant shows that she is objective. Clear line and word spacing show that she is well organized.

Dominant lower zones

Upright slant

"Gatsby turned out all right at th

pueyed on Gatsby, what foul dust

of his dreams (that temporarily c

The Great Gatsby   F. Scott

There are moments on most days when I feel a deep and sincere gratitude, when I sit at the open window, and there is a blue sky or moving clouds.

Large letter size

FULL OF LIFE SAMPLE

Thick pen stroke

nd; it is what
ated in the wake
at my interest......"

lzgerald.

ANALYTICAL SAMPLE

Full of Life

The sample above reveals an individual who is full of life and good company. This writer has a thick pen stroke, indicating that she has vitality, and that her appreciation for beauty is seen in the way she uses all her senses to enjoy life. Large letter size is another expression of her ability to visualize future projects creatively. Although she appreciates good company, she prefers to have a good chat with one friend at a time. This is shown by the wide spaces between words.

Pen Stroke • 3

Picture the writer

Thick pen strokes indicate a jovial personality, while thin strokes reveal a quieter character.

People who like to make thick strokes on paper are easygoing, enjoy socializing, and have many and varied interests. They buy the best thay can because they appreciate high quality.

Often people who enjoy writing with thick strokes have their own special fountain pen, and they will want to use that for day-to-day writing and for their sample. They may even refuse to use a disposable or ballpoint pen. If they cannot use their preferred broad nib to produce a thick stroke, they may choose to use a pencil instead.

Positive application

You may hear someone who produces a thick stroke before you see them as they let forth a good gusty laugh in a restaurant. This person will enjoy the best quality of wine that they can afford and will be good company at the dinner table. They may well also have a vast amount of general knowledge in a variety of areas because they have so many interests and hobbies. To the writer with a thick pen stroke, sophistication could well mean bright hues, embellishments, and grandeur.

People who like to write with a thin stroke are often self-disciplined and determined. They may well be experts in one or two areas and will have an enormous store of in-depth information on their specialty subject. Clothes such people wear may be in pastel shades, which are discreet yet elegant, refined, and genteel.

While many people enjoy beauty in the form of paintings, the person who likes to make thick pen strokes will probably prefer brightly colored pictures showing plenty of activity. The kind of writer who enjoys making thin pen strokes may well prefer a spring landscape that has been rendered in pastel colors.

There are many people who do not mind whether the pen strokes they produce are thick or thin. These people will have a diverse visual taste; they will enjoy some bright colors as well as pastel shades. In conversation, they may offer their general views, rather than have strong opinions, about paintings and other objects of visual beauty. In this day and age when modern society is in a rush and everything is done at speed, it is becoming quite common for people to use any pen that is available as long as it contains ink. On the other hand, artists and those who are acutely affected by pen stroke width will usually carry their own pens. In time, this may begin to have even more significance than it does at present in society. The computer may save a lot of writing, but there will always be pens for sale.

PEN STROKE • 4

It is important that a pen and not a pencil is used for writing a sample for analysis. A pencil tip changes constantly, because the point becomes blunt and then fine again once it has been sharpened. This will give a false picture of the width of someone's handwriting stroke as well as of the pressure they use while writing. When people are adamant about writing only in pencil, make a note of this and perhaps ask for two samples to be written, one in pencil and the other in pen.

Balanced

As we have already observed, many people use the nearest pen and do not worry about the thickness of their pen strokes. This writing sample shows a healthy balance between being too sensitive and too easygoing. The writer has neither pasty nor sharp writing. It is balanced in other ways also, such as clear line spacing, which indicates her organizational skills. With its legible writing, the sample indicates that the person is keen to communicate in an articulate manner. The narrowness of the width between the letters reflects her determination to see a task all the way through to its conclusion.

Clear line space

C'est en première réussis enfin à place. M'étant a dispose à achete sans savoir au j comment m) pren

Perfect wisdom have four parts, viz.;
wisdom, the principle of doing things aright;
Justice the principle of doing things
equally in public and private; fortitude the
principle of not flying danger, but meeting
it; and temperance, the principle of
subduing desires and living moderately, -

Plato

Rising line ends
Rising line starts

QUALITY SAMPLE

que je
...tenir une
...sig Il me
...mon biller,
...é, cependant,
...e.

BALANCED SAMPLE

Narrow width

Quality in All Spheres

The thick nib that has been used here is very evident. This reflects that quality in all areas of life is very important to this writer. He will give his best and he would like to receive the best. The heavy pressure shows that he works hard, and the narrowness indicates his single-minded determination to achieve his goals. A slightly rising baseline reflects his optimistic outlook on life.

Letter Forms • 1

Your determination shows

Writers who display an angular letter formation will be keen to achieve the goals they have set themselves.

If you look at an individual letter that a writer writes you will see that it is often either one line, or a combination of two lines—a straight line and a curved line. When two straight lines meet, they make an angle. If one continuous line goes around a corner, it makes a curve. The way we form these two lines is an indication of our basic attitude to life. The more angles we have, the more determined we are, and the more curves we have, the more gentle is our manner. It is interesting to note that some samples contain the same kind of letter formation throughout, while others do not. Not only will some have a mixture of letter forms, but some will have garlands that look different each time they are produced.

The balance

A healthy mix of angles and curves in someone's handwriting shows that the writer can be both tenacious and empathetic. The writer knows when to use persistence and when to be compassionate. The more that the angle can be seen in the handwriting, the more determined the writer is to succeed. The amount of curve in evidence indicates the amount of kindness that the writer displays toward others. When a curve is found at the top of parallel lines, it is called an arcade; this identifies people who are tactful and diplomatic. People who are able to turn the two parallel lines into one wavy line are inclined to want to keep their options open for as long as possible. These letter forms are often found in the handwriting of people who are good at negotiating.

Making different letter forms

Let us take the formation of the lower case "n." Visualize two parallel lines. Join them together with a rounded curve at the top and this will give you an arcade letter form. Imagine another set of parallel lines; this time make a curve to join them at the bottom, and this will give you a garland. When you see the letter "n" written as a "u," that is a garland formation. Think again about the two parallel lines. This time, in order to keep the lines straight, they are going to have to change direction, thus creating an angle, hence the angular formation. Finally, a wavy line is created when the parallel lines turn into one undulating line. When a wavy line disintegrates and loses its form, the professional analyst will note it down as a "thread."

Letter Forms: The Key

Garlands indicate an individual who is friendly, easygoing, and empathetic. Arcades show a person who is protective and good at keeping secrets, and also loves tradition. Angles indicate someone who is industrious and determined; this person will always need to complete the task. Wavy lines imply that their writer is flexible, and a good mediator who likes to keep their options open.

LETTER FORMS • 2

When looking at a lower case letter "n" it can sometimes be difficult to see if the movement at the top of the letter is actually a curve or an angle. Using a disposable pen that has run out of ink to trace over the sample can be very helpful in these cases. You may have to follow the script of the writer for several lines until you find out whether the pen is curving around at the top of the letter "n" or whether it is actually stopping and changing direction.

Determination

The angular letter forms reflect the determination of this writer to succeed. Her right slant and firm pressure show that she will persevere to the end, however challenging the task. Note the long strokes that are found at the beginning of most of the words. This shows that she likes to prepare herself for whatever she is going to do. With the right slant of emotion and the connectedness of letters, this individual makes judgements that are sometimes emotional and at other times logical.

Long starting stroke

In family
the oil that
friction, the
binds closer
the music t
harmony.

General

122

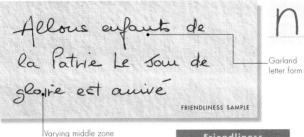

Garland
letter form

FRIENDLINESS SAMPLE

Varying middle zone

Friendliness

In this sample, the garland is beautifully illustrated—especially in the word "enfants," where the letter "n" looks just like the letter "u." The friendliness of the rounded movements is supported by the slightly rising baselines, which reflect a positive outlook on life. The gentle left slant indicates the importance of family life to the person and the variation in the middle slant shows the adaptability of this writer to fit in with other people and to be flexible in different situations.

Marked right slant

DETERMINATION SAMPLE

Letter Forms • 3

Curves and angles

Those who work in the caring professions are most likely to write using a garland formation.

There are an infinite number of combinations that make up letter forms. This is one of the reasons why a comprehensive computer program cannot be put together for analyzing handwriting. We are all unique, and, while a certain amount of determination and friendliness are helpful when dealing with life to achieve some of our goals, we also make many choices, not least about our attitude, and also about how we set out to meet others and fit in or make the most of life that we can.

When you look at a piece of writing and cannot decide whether it has more angles or more curves, then they are probably in balance. This means that the writer will have a healthy determination for achievement but will also know when to let go and have a break and relax. To back up your observations, feel the pressure of the writing sample to make sure it is firm. If broadness is also present, then you will know you have analyzed the handwriting correctly.

Sometimes a writing sample will not be balanced and will show only angles or curves. If the letters are angular, this indicates that the writer's energies go into achieving goals. If they are rounded, the writer's energy is used for helping others.

Positive application

Writers who create angles in their sample put real effort into everything they do. They tend to be self-disciplined and have the ability to persevere through each obstacle as it arises in their determination to succeed and achieve their preset goal. They are able to summon up great courage at times of crisis and are prepared to take risks in order to overcome the dangers that impede progress.

Individuals who write with garlands are kind, sympathetic, and usually understanding toward others. They are often found in the caring professions, since they have endless patience and a genuine desire to help others, whether emotionally or on a practical level. These writers may have a natural flair for tact and diplomacy. They can keep a secret and would rather bend the truth than hurt someone's feelings.

Those who write with a lot of wavy-line letter forms usually enjoy mediating. Their ability is to be flexible and to compromise, particularly in difficult situations, and they have a natural flair for showing understanding to parties on both sides in a conflict. However grave the deadlock, they can help to find a solution that will be acceptable to all parties.

LETTER FORMS • 4

One of the handwriting movements that indicates determination is angular letter formation. However, in order to support the idea that they have stamina and persistence, these writers will need to display firm pressure. This is just one example of why it is necessary to observe several different writing movements with the same interpretation before one can be sure of an accurate analysis. When samples contain angular letter forms made with light pressure, their writers may talk in a very determined way, but will lack the energy for sustained action.

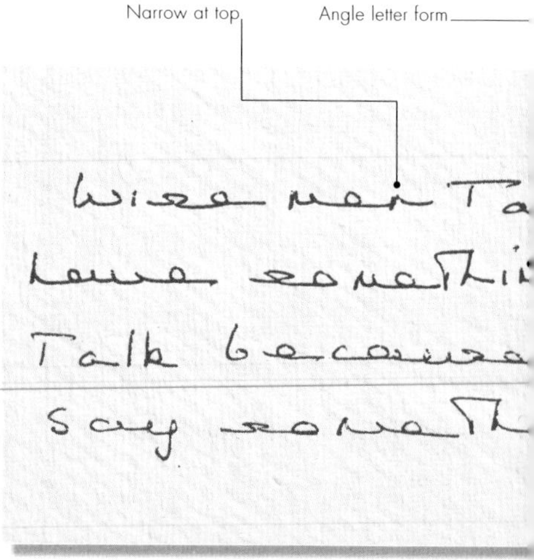

Narrow at top

Angle letter form

Logical

The angles in this writing show the determination and ability of this writer to keep going until a task is completed. Look at the way the letter "n" is formed. There is a very narrow angle at the top which branches out to become wider at the bottom of the second stroke. This shows her ability to focus on a project and to apply herself completely and absolutely to the cause of the moment.

People who buy newly-built homes can end up receiving a worse after-sales service than when buying a washing machine.

Sunday Telegraph July 16 2000

EMPATHETIC SAMPLE

| Wavy line

because they ... to say; fools ... hey have to ... g — Plato

LOGICAL SAMPLE

Empathetic

This sample shows a fascinating combination of letter forms. The predominantly wavy-line appearance shows that this writer is flexible and empathetic. The heavy pressure and the rounded garland letter forms show that she prefers to communicate in a gentle yet firm way. Where there is conflict, she prefers to mediate to achieve a result that is workable to all parties. This is time-consuming and tiring for her, but she is able to give the impression to both parties in a conflict that she has their genuine interests and long-term goals in mind.

Margins • 1

Four margins to interpret
*Well laid-out margins show
someone who is able to get
along well with other people.*

There are four margins on a page, and each one has its own significance. The upper margin indicates how important the aesthetic value of things is to the writer. It also indicates their attitude toward their own economic circumstances. The larger the upper margins become, the easier the writer finds it to spend money. A wide lower margin indicates their ability to make decisions. The closer the last line of the writing to the end of the page, the more these writers prefer to postpone making decisions.

The left margin indicates the importance of the past in our lives today. The closer that our writing clings to the left margin, the more we will base our future decisions on our past experiences. The further away from the edge of the paper we choose to make the left margin, the keener we are to go forward and leave the past behind.

The right margin signifies our attitude toward the future. A narrow right margin that has writing close to the edge of the page indicates an individual who is keen to move forward. A wider margin shows that we are apprehensive about what lies over the horizon.

The balance

When all margins are laid out well on a page, it shows that we are usually able to make good use of our time and talents. We also get along with other people and fit in with our environment. Balanced margins on all sides of the paper show a certain inner self-discipline as well as aesthetic taste.

How to judge margins

Deciding whether a margin is large or small depends on the size of a page and how the rest of the space on the paper has been used. Sometimes one margin will be visibly larger or smaller than the other margins, and this will help you to determine the size of the other margins.

The top margin is not always open to interpretation. When people write on headed notepaper, the upper margin has already been chosen for them. However, the position of writing from the top of the second piece of paper can give a good indication of the true upper margin.

Margins: The Key

Wide left margins indicate individuals who are keen to leave the past behind. Narrow left margins reveal people for whom family values are important, and for whom past experiences form the basis for decision-making. Wide right margins show individuals experiencing a temporary phase of uncertainty. Narrow right margins indicate people who are keen to go forward and taste the future.

MARGINS · 2

Determining margins is one of the reasons why samples need to be written on paper 8½ x 11 inches. This gives the writers sufficient space to choose their own margins without being cramped. When samples are written on small pieces of paper, it is sometimes safer to ignore the margins—this will prevent mistakes in the interpretation. When analyzing handwriting, quality is vital at all times. It is far wiser to produce a short and accurate portrait of the writer than to produce a long report with errors.

Challenges

The writer of this sample enjoys being with people. The very tight right margin shows that she is always ready for something new. The dominance of the middle zone shows that she is a practical person who lives for today and is able to change and adapt her priorities as and when necessary.

Horizontal mingling

Dominant middle zone

Garland letter form

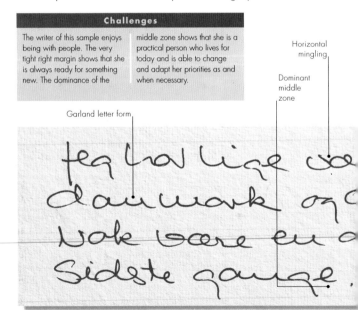

Thy yesterday is
thy past; thy today
thy future; thy
tomorrow is thy
secret.
The best preache
is the heart; the
best teacher is
time; the best book
in the world; the
best friend is God.

Connected
letters

SELF-DISCIPLINE SAMPLE

Self-Discipline

The straightness of this
left margin shows that
the writer can exercise
self-discipline when
required. Her mainly-
connected writing with
an upright slant
indicates that she takes
a commonsense
approach to life.

Upright slant

l i
t cil
de

CHALLENGES SAMPLE

Margins • 3

Size and position

Margins must be judged from a sample written on 8½ x 11 inches paper in order to be accurate.

The size and positioning of margins is decided at an unconscious level. In handwriting analysis, the page represents the writer's own environment, and how they perceive themselves within it is displayed as they spontaneously fill the page with writing.

Margins are, of course, a major factor in the general layout of the page. So, we can deduce that the more balanced they appear to be, the easier it has been for the writer to keep different parts of their life in proper proportion to each other. Knowing when to relax, when to use self-restraint, and when to let go are all part of maintaining a balanced lifestyle.

Margins may vary in appearance on different samples of writing by the same person, depending on several factors. Take the simplest instance: if the paper is very small, there simply is not room for the margins normally preferred.

A more complex reason may be a stressful situation which makes the writer anxious about the future—perhaps a new job, starting a new life, or going through a period of grieving. These are all temporary situations where the unconscious takes over and influences the difference in the margin spacing. You may find that letters written during such times have right margins much wider than in a writer's usual style, because the right margin indicates an individual's attitude to the future.

Positive application

When you see the left margin going straight down the page without wavering, it indicates good self-discipline. Sometimes people who are very creative and have generally irregular writing will nevertheless write with a straight left margin. It is a sign that they can use self-discipline when they need to, but that—as a rule—they prefer to use their energy in a spontaneous, creative, and rather individual way.

The average right margin is jagged, depending on how many letters there are in the final word in each line. This kind of margin shows that the writer has a healthy approach to the future and is ready to take on any challenges that they might encounter.

Margins are interesting because, although they are usually made unconsciously, sometimes the writer will have to compromise on margin size when a piece of paper is small and the message that the writer wants to convey is large. In this case, the true margin might not show. If the writer can maintain a straight left margin, however, then there is a great deal of self-discipline present.

MARGINS • 4

Sometimes you will see a left margin increasing in size as it makes its way down the page. In order to decide whether this means that the writer is cautious when first meeting people, or is suffering from fatigue, it is necessary to check the pressure. When firm pressure is present, the individual will tend to be cautious upon meeting people for the first time, while, when the pressure is light, the writer will be tired.

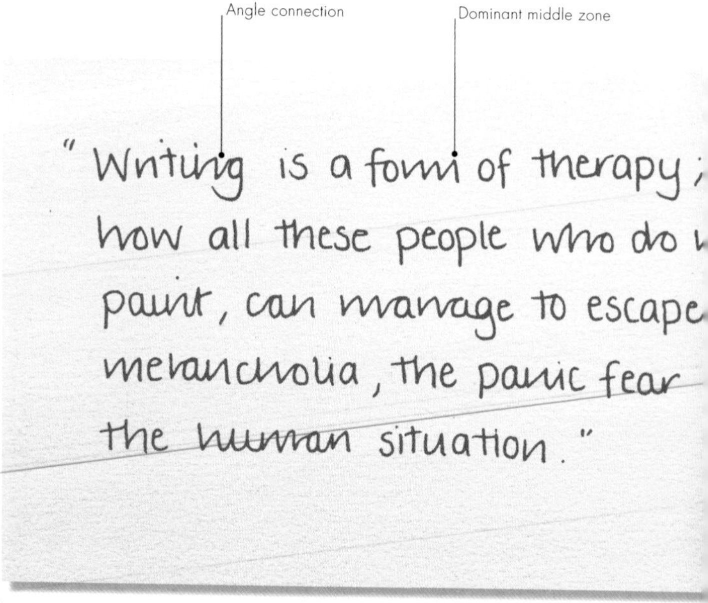

Angle connection

Dominant middle zone

" Writing is a form of therapy;
how all these people who do
paint, can manage to escape
melancholia, the panic fear
the human situation. "

Disciplined

The lady who has written this has a clear, regular, neat style, which shows a disciplined approach to life. However, it is interesting to see how the left margin gradually widens on each successive line. This shows that she is cautious at first, but when she acclimatizes to new surroundings, she then feels more at ease. The middle zone is so regular that it differs less than a fraction of an inch throughout.

Arcade form

Regular middle zone

ometimes I wonder

t write, compose or

ne madness, the

hich is inherent in

Graham Greene, P444/25

DISCIPLINED SAMPLE

Summary

I am seques

Look for dominant signs
The importance of finding three different movements to support your interpretation is paramount.

We have now looked at the major handwriting signs. When they are observed correctly, an accurate analysis of the personality can be undertaken.

When looking at handwriting samples, note which movements you are able to recognize immediately. This will help you to determine the dominant signs correctly. If in doubt about deciding the nature of a particular symbol, leave it out. It is far better to be accurate by using fewer handwriting movements than to hazard a guess at all the signs present and make mistakes.

Expert analysts can deduce a lot about a writer's personality using just the pressure, spacing, and rhythm.

For each of your interpretations to be correct, it is essential to make sure that three different handwriting movements with the same meaning are present in the writing. For instance, the following signs show ambition: rising baselines, heavy pressure, and large size. There are other signs that signify ambition, such as a right slant, connectedness, and angles. However, three different movements are enough for the purposes of interpretation.

The "dead pen"

If you have difficulty deciding what movements are present, try using the dead pen technique and tracing carefully and exactly over the writing movements of the sample. This can help you to determine the difference between such movements as an angle and a curve. Sometimes it can be difficult to decide whether the letter form is an arcade or angle. After using the dead pen for a few minutes, if you have followed the sample carefully, you will either have come to a stop and had to change direction, or the pen will have made a continuous and rounded movement at the top of the upstroke.

The more accurate you can be in your assessment and notation of the writing movements, the more likely you are to analyze someone's personality correctly. Mistakes may occur at two particular stages during the analysis.

The first is when the handwriting movements present in the sample are incorrectly described. When you look up the interpretations, they will be wrong as a result.

The second place where it is possible to make a mistake is when insufficient supporting movements are used to back up the interpretation. Handwriting analysis is a deductive science. This means that one movement by itself has no meaning.

If you want to analyze handwriting regularly, it is a good idea to establish a regular working method covering first impressions, detailed observation, the collation of the information, and the production of an accurate report.

HOW TO
PUT IT TOGETHER

Now that you have learned to recognize the main writing movements, you can begin to find the correct interpretations. Handwriting analysis is a useful tool in many different areas. In business, it may be used in the selection of job candidates; when more than one candidate is suitable for the job, handwriting can show which person will best fit in with the existing team. Handwriting analysis may also be useful in problem solving, building working relationships, and developing promotion prospects. It can be a tool for choosing careers: teenagers leaving high school, young adults at university, and those seeking a new career direction can use handwriting analysis to point them in the right direction.

Practical
Sample Analysis

First things first

List the movements that you can recognize and their interpretations.

Make a note of the movements in the sample on page 142. You will see that these movements are present: clear line spacing; garland letter forms, mainly slanting slightly to the right; irregular spacing between words; thin strokes; fluctuating letter size in the middle zone; mainly disconnected letters with some connectedness; stable baselines; some flowing rhythm; and a margin that enlarges on the right-hand side.

Now think about the interpretations. Beside each movement, make a note of the general interpretation. To be sure you are correct, always choose three

different movements with the same meaning. Make some working notes to help you. Remember, line spacing tells us about order. The whole layout of the sample is clear, and the firm pressure applied shows the writer has enough energy to plan her life. The letter forms are garlanded, indicating a friendly and empathetic person. The varying middle zone supports this, as does the occasional rightward slant.

The slant, mixed word spacing, and varying middle zone are all indications that the writer enjoys socializing. Her thin pen stroke shows that she has an analytical mind; this is supported by the simplified stroke. The varying middle zone and letters which are sometimes connected show that she is practical and enjoys variety. The baselines are fairly stable; this movement is complementary to the slight right slant and the rhythm, which all show that she enjoys inner harmony. Irregularity shows that she can be flexible.

Put it together

The writer has an organized approach to life. She is an analytical thinker who is practical, sociable, flexible, and empathetic, and she enjoys variety.

Key to Interpretation	
clear line spacing	clarity of plans and thoughts
letter forms	attitude to life (garland = friendly)
upright varying slant	emotional expression fairly balanced
word spacing mixed	social needs
thin pen stroke	sensitivity
varying middle zone	practicality
connectedness	logical/intuitive thinking
baselines fairly stable	emotional mood of the moment
rhythm	amount of inner harmony present
irregularity	flexibility

PRACTICAL SAMPLE ANALYSIS • 2

The sample below relates to the detailed analysis that was discussed on pages 140–41. Look closely at the handwriting and see whether you can recognize the movements that were listed there. Don't worry if they are not all immediately apparent. You will find that the longer you practice handwriting analysis, the better you will become at seeing the more subtle movements.

Social Worker

The woman who wrote this sample is actually a social worker. When we go back through the interpretation of her handwriting movements, we can see that she has many of the qualities that are necessary for such a position. She has an effective, organized approach, as shown in her clear line and word spacing. Her simplified style shows that she can use analytical thinking for practical purposes. While she enjoys socializing and has a generally empathetic approach to others, she is also able to take firm decisions when she is required to do so. The irregularity of her writing shows that she is flexible and can change her priorities at short notice.

Slight rightward slant

Stable baseline

Clear word and line spacing

SOCIAL WORKER

Handwriting Analysis in Careers

Assessment
Handwriting analysis is one of the tools that you can use to assess your professional qualities.

Handwriting analysis is a useful tool in assisting people to find a suitable career. Whether a person is graduating from high school or college, looking for a second career in their 30s or 40s, or seeking a new challenge in their 50s and 60s, handwriting analysis can find unexplored avenues.

Handwriting analysis can be beneficial in showing the strengths of the writer, and positive and practical in helping to boost the self-esteem. It may be helpful, particularly in the case of people who have been laid off, to meet the writers and go through the analysis with them. By talking through their situation and reinforcing their strengths and potential, they can begin to feel hopeful and optimistic about their future. A plan of action can then be made, and often they will not only succeed in their new choice of career, but they will also be a lot happier in their new job than they were before.

Background information

Before embarking on such an analysis, it is useful for the analyst to be given some background information about the client. For instance, the analyst will need to know what qualifications the client has, and whether he or she is undertaking any courses. It is also important for the analyst to know what time and budget the client has available in order to pursue a new career path, what other commitments he or she has, and how much the client is actually willing to change. It may also be useful to know what their general interests are and what hobbies they pursue. Other issues, such as disability, may be relevant too. If a writer is considering a new post, a job description is helpful. Remember that starting a new career requires energy, fortitude, and commitment.

At the outset, it is helpful for the analyst to know what sort of help a writer is looking for, and how they think that having their handwriting analyzed will assist them. It may be that a writer has several ideas for new careers, and needs guidance to make the best choice. Some writers have already made up their minds and simply want confirmation that they have the qualities to succeed. Others are sent by parents or supervisors to have their writing analyzed for any number of reasons. There are those who say they want career guidance, but in fact need emotional counseling. There are so many possible reasons that it is important for you to find out the writer's real motive for pursuing the analysis before you start.

Part-time work

Artistic skills can improve the quality of your life in many different ways.

ARTISTIC DESIGNER • 1
This writer came for advice on her future. She wanted to work from home, because she had various commitments that prevented her from doing a nine-to-five job in an office. She wanted to use her skills, but was unavailable to work full time, and did not want to commit herself to working for an organization. She wanted to know if she could work on her own, how best to use her talents, and to become aware of the areas in which she could develop her potential.

Original style

Creative connection

Hiflos suchte ich in meinen Taschen nach Zigaretten, obwohl ich wusste, dass ich keine mehr hatte, wohl noch eine Packung im Auto lag, aber das Auto stand zwanzig Meter rechts von der Haustür, und etwas wie ein Ozean lag zwischen mir und dem Auto.

Spontaneous

The spontaneous rhythm and original style show that this writer is creative. Her pen stroke is an interesting mixture, showing that texture, color, and variety are important to her. The fairly simplified writing and clear layout show that she would be able to think on her feet and produce some original ideas when time is limited, but be flexible enough to implement changes, if required, at short notice.

Raring to go

Starting a different career can open up a whole new life.

Artistic Designer • 2

Check your vocation
*To ensure your future happiness,
it is important to choose work
that satisfies you.*

This designer wanted to work to fulfill her creative potential. Her children had left home, her husband traveled a fair amount, and she did some voluntary work. She was full of creative ideas and often found herself looking at the decor in social situations. This gave her the desire to put her thoughts into action.

Realizing her potential in a work situation would bring this writer all-round benefits. The possibility of achieving hitherto unthought-of goals and dreams and the happiness she would find in spending time doing a job that would bring her satisfaction in this area were very important to her.

Instant decision
Given her skills, several different careers would have suited this writer. However, it is always important to take personal inclination into account. At the mention of artistic design, her eyes lit up, her voice brightened, and she decided instantly that it was what she would like to do. Different avenues of working in artistic design were then discussed, as well as the practical side of running her own business. While she could be self-employed, she would need a partner to run the office and the accounting side of the enterprise. Her strengths would lie in visiting clients in their homes, and matching design and color schemes with the personalities of the owners.

The excitement she gained from the idea of being stimulated to reach out to challenges, understand, and more importantly, provide clients with a high quality product that would bring constant admiration from everyone, appeared to make this the right path for this writer.

She will benefit from going on a course to learn about the different aspects of being self-employed. It can be daunting at first; most of us are apt to be intimidated by the prospect of managing our own business, particularly where financial and taxation issues are concerned. However, acquiring these new skills, mixing with other people who are in the process of starting their own businesses, and learning how to keep customers happy will become second nature to her in the course of time. Going on a course will also help her to network. In addition, she will have her tutors on hand to offer helpful advice, should she need any assistance in the early days.

Once all of this painstaking preparatory work has been undertaken and she begins to feel more confident, she will then be able to build a capable team around her whose members will be able to cooperate and work well together. In this way, she should be able to manage all the different aspects of starting a business.

Instability
Being laid off may seem negative, but it is an opportunity for reassessment.

CUSTOMER RELATIONS • 1

This writer had been laid off because the office where she had been working was closed when a larger company bought out a similar type of business in the same town. Her confidence had understandably been knocked by being unemployed, so before applying for a new job in a slightly different direction, she wanted to make sure that she would be suitable for the post.

Disconnected letters

Connected letters

Excess on occasion is exhilarating. It prevents moderation from acquiring the deadening effect of habit.

W. Somerset Maugham

Empathy

This writer has upright writing, reflecting a practical approach to life. With some letters joined while others are disconnected, she may have intuitive ideas, which can then be backed up logically. Her wide word spacing allows her to work alone or to fit into a team. The garlands in her writing reflect her kindness and empathy in dealing with other people. The ability to think on her feet, change priorities when new situations arise, and be practical are all characteristics that are part of her character and can be seen in the natural spontaneity of the writing flow.

Back to school

To change your career path, you may need to concentrate on learning new skills.

Customer Relations • 2

Change of course
*Consulting a analyst can
give an insight into talents that may
be put to use in the future.*

This person was tempted to consult an analyst when she saw an advertisement in the local paper for a customer services agent job. The description indicated that the vacancy was in the local branch of a large organization. The skills required by the position included dealing with customers' queries over the counter, as well as on the telephone, and via email. Some letter writing was also involved. Training would be given in the computer programs used by the company; however, a knowledge of basic computing skills would be a definite asset. There would be some shift work, and there would be good promotional prospects for the candidate with the right skills.

The writer had enjoyed the variety of transactions and the process of dealing with customers that she had handled across the counter in her previous occupation, and, while she wanted to be less involved with number work, the idea of customer services was certainly worth exploring.

Other potential

While considering the prospects of a career in customer relations, this person's writing also indicates that she has the talent to succeed in other areas. She is a teamworker and willing to learn new skills. Her flexibility and common sense mean that several new careers could beckon, and this need not be her first choice.

When a client comes for help in finding a career, there are some things that cannot be gleaned from their handwriting. For instance, on meeting this writer it became apparent that her interests lie mostly in the present. While she may not have thought what she might like to be doing in ten years' time, the analyst may be able to plan a course of action for her so that she may develop her career in a way which could be useful to her. However, whether this woman will want to plan that far ahead is another matter; people who enjoy living in the present are often reluctant to do this.

If she could be persuaded to verbalize her unacknowledged dreams, she might become more aware of how her potential could be satisfyingly fulfilled. However, if she prefers to continue to live mainly in the present tense, then the analyst should respect her choice.

Key: Positive People Skills

These are indicated by a mixture of all the letter forms, medium–heavy pressure, upright or rightward slant, average width, and half-and-half connectedness.

Diverse
The profession of accounting actually includes many different types of job.

ACCOUNTANT • 1

This man took time out after going to college, because he wanted to travel and was otherwise unsure what to do with his life. He visited many countries and worked wherever he could find a job. He found that he had a flair for managing his money. When he returned home, he considered becoming an accountant and sought advice from an analyst about which branch of accounting to pursue.

Connected   Wide word space   Left slant   Disconnected

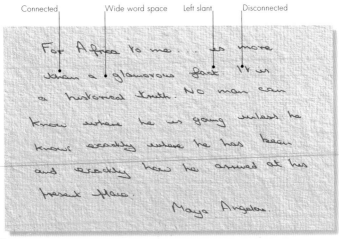

For Africa to me ... is more
than a glamorous fact. It is
a historical truth. No man can
know where he is going unless he
knows exactly where he has been
and exactly how he arrived at his
present place.

Maya Angelou.

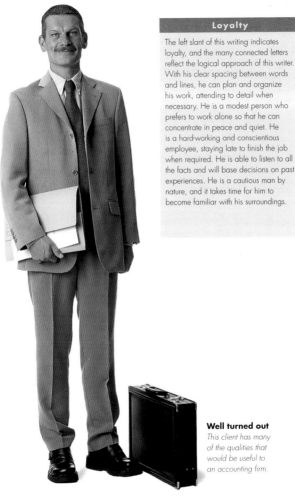

Loyalty

The left slant of this writing indicates loyalty, and the many connected letters reflect the logical approach of this writer. With his clear spacing between words and lines, he can plan and organize his work, attending to detail when necessary. He is a modest person who prefers to work alone so that he can concentrate in peace and quiet. He is a hard-working and conscientious employee, staying late to finish the job when required. He is able to listen to all the facts and will base decisions on past experiences. He is a cautious man by nature, and it takes time for him to become familiar with his surroundings.

Well turned out

This client has many of the qualities that would be useful to an accounting firm.

Accountant • 2

Home or away?
*Many careers offer a variety of
working environments, specializations,
and modes of working.*

Accounting is a profession that covers an enormous spectrum and offers a wide variety of fields in which to specialize. Some accountants like to travel and enjoy the investigative side of the profession, while others prefer the stability of going to work in the same place every day.

It is important to establish that high school graduates are not going into accounting just to follow their family tradition. This can lead to early frustration in an unsuitable career when a different choice could provide satisfaction. Some areas of accounting require communication skills and an ability to deal with the public, while in other fields one can work alone on individual tasks that do not require great social skills.

Solitary worker

The writing sample of the accountant on pages 154–55 shows that this man enjoys working alone and, when he meets people, he prefers to do so on a one-to-one basis. He is a good listener but he finds it difficult to stop other people from talking; it will be important to establish how much time he is willing to spend working with clients and how much time he needs to spend on his own. His travels have given him some confidence, and so he feels that he would like to have a certain amount of client contact. He has a thorough approach, so he would be good at detailed auditing; his patience and listening skills will be useful in collecting information from clients. He will feel safer working for a large public company, where he will not have to worry about acquiring all of the skills necessary to self-employment, and where he will enjoy a variety of tasks. He would appreciate the challenge of being part of a team involved in share valuations and company mergers. Another great advantage of working for a large corporation is that it provides the opportunity to develop new skills in the chosen career path. Also, there are always plenty of other employees available when a new recruit is seeking guidance.

Taxation is another branch of the accounting profession that might interest this client; this would require him to advise a range of clients on the best ways for them to minimize their taxation bills. Insolvency is another field that he might be interested in; this kind of work involves investigating the situations of financially precarious companies. However, when environmental auditing (the process of investigating a company's environmental impact) was mentioned, this client decided that he would pursue this course.

Smooth talker

A talented salesperson should be able to sell ice to the Inuit.

SALESPERSON • 1

This woman is very happy with her job in a large sales company, but she is ready for a change and is considering setting up on her own. She came to an analyst to see whether she had the skills that she would need to do this. Although she has a proven track record in sales, becoming self-employed would require that she learn some new skills and perhaps consider one or two areas of weakness.

Very large size

Marked slant to the right

I like men to behave
strong and childish

On the Move

This large handwriting and its flowing rightward slant indicate a writer who is keen to move forward, likes to be with people, and has the drive to sell. The pen stroke is thin and some of the letters connected, showing that the writer uses an analytical and logical approach when communicating with a prospective customer. The pressure on the page is light, indicating that she enjoys having an assistant to work with her and keep paperwork up to date. This writer enjoys the challenge of selling and is keen to plan and organize her schedule to see as many clients as possible every day.

Confident

There are many different ways to be successful in sales.

Salesperson • 2

Patient
A job that involves "cold calling" requires a calm personality with lots of patience.

There is no single handwriting style that denotes the perfect salesperson. When so many types of selling are possible, different skills are needed for different situations. Sitting on the end of a telephone all day cold calling requires a lot of discipline. Going out into the field when you know that a client is interested in your product can be very rewarding. With a lot of traveling between customers, however, the working day may be very long and arduous. A lot of stamina will be required.

Extroverts who rely on their personality to sell often have a rightward slant and large handwriting, while introverts may have a left slant and small writing with wide word spacing. Extroverts will prefer to go into the client's environment and get to know the person who has purchasing authority. Having established themselves, these sales people will then go and find the products or services needed by the client. They are great fun and exude confidence. They have an ability to make others feel at ease and this is how they achieve their success in sales.

It can happen that the more dynamic the salesperson, the less they enjoy paperwork. In this case it will be essential to find someone who will work with them as part of a team.

Empathetic personality

The handwriting of the woman on pages 158–59 shows that she has many of the skills that are required for a successful career in sales. She loves variety and she enjoys being the boss.

She believes that if she ran her own company she would be completely in charge; however, it is important to remember that there is a big difference between running one department in a large company, and being responsible for all the departments of a one-woman business. She may be wiser to look at other ways of exploiting her skills. She oozes dynamism and friendliness, and she has the ability to make her clients feel that she has all the time in the world for them. She also has a great memory for personal details, such as her clients' leisure interests and the names of their partners and children. This woman also has a lot of self-confidence, which is vital to a successful sales career.

Because she enjoys variety and new challenges, she would probably be happiest if she moved to a new post in another company. Or, she might prefer to learn a new set of skills that would enable her to work in a new area of sales. She would gain satisfaction from being involved in the design of a product from its earliest inception.

Vulnerable
*This client has the skills
that are necessary for
the care of animals.*

VETERINARY NURSE • 1 This 40-year-old man
decided to see an analyst when he decided on a change of career after a
long period in the same job. By analyzing his handwriting, the analyst will be
able to identify his character traits and point him in the right direction for an
entirely new career.

Left slant   Loops

She was held in custody
for ten months pending trial,
and was then sentenced to
four years, suspended.

MALE:- "Stalkers" by
Jea Ritchie.

Organization

The writer of this sample produces a leftward slant, showing loyalty, and a mixture of letter forms, which reflects his adaptable approach. The clear line spacing shows his ability to plan and organize, and the firm pressure shows his determination to complete the training and persevere through difficult challenges as and when they arise. The thickness of the pen stroke means that the writer will give his best, and his future employers will be pleased with his thorough approach to work and also his kindness to animals. The loops in the upper zone show that he has ideas and the loops in the lower zone indicate that he can turn the ideas into successful action and achieve his goals.

Self-effacing
People who enjoy peace and quiet will not be well suited to working in very competitive environments.

Veterinary Nurse • 2

Unhappy at work?
*Seeing a analyst to consider
your career options is one way to
put a spring into your step.*

This client had been working for 20 years in a technical position at a local college. This career had demanded a lot of precision and concentration and, now that he had reached the age of 40, he decided that he would like to effect a complete change in his life by switching to a different kind of job. Analysis of his handwriting sample shows that he is a practical person and that he often helps out his friends and neighbors with any general maintenance problems they may be having. His is a gentle and

kind personality, perhaps not best suited to a business where a forceful approach is required. If he wanted to become a maintenance engineer, for instance, it would be wiser to join a small firm where the worries of running the business and dealing with awkward customers would be the responsibility of someone else.

A dog's life

Listening to how he loves his dog and enjoys walking for long distances prompted the suggestion about working with animals and several possibilities were discussed.

Admittance to vet school is highly competitive and places are few. The writer decided he would prefer to train as a veterinary nurse. When qualified he could gain confidence gently while working under the experienced eyes of a veterinarian.

It was important to have some form of income while training. The most practical way forward, which would allow him to earn while he trained, was to change direction by taking on two different tasks simultaneously. He would study to become a veterinary nurse and, to help pay for the course, he would offer a professional dog-walking service. Once he had gained the necessary qualification, he would be able to earn a living by using his new knowledge and skills.

Support

His wife was delighted with his choice, and willing to help and support him in whatever ways were necessary. She would act as a backup to ensure that the dog-walking service worked efficiently and reliably. By taking the risk and having the support of his wife, this writer has enhanced his self-esteem, and his marriage is even more rewarding than it was before.

Changing careers at the age of 40 and starting completely afresh may take some courage, especially when a new course of training and examinations will be required before the desired qualification can be attained.

Different speeds

On entering a career, not everyone has the same goals.

PROMOTION • 1

When a promotion is handled well, it can lead to satisfaction in many ways, both for the person who has been promoted as well as the supervisor, the team, and the organization. We all work and advance at different speeds. Some of us are keen to rise quickly, while others may need encouragement to apply for a promotion.

Common sense

L'Angleterre, ah, la perfide Angleterre, que le rempart de ses mers rendoit inaccessible aux Romains, la foi du Sauveur y est abordée.

Jacques-Bénigne Bossuet

Friendliness

Team Leader

The writer of this sample is able to work well in a team. The firm pressure and the upright slant of her handwriting indicate that she has a practical approach and works hard. The garlands show a friendly and empathetic personality, and the close word spacing shows that she enjoys socializing and being part of a team—and may make a good team leader. She is modest, so she may need some persuasion to take on this role. Once she decides to put her name forward, she would commit herself to the new position, learning the required new skills and taking on the relevant responsibilities. Her flexibility allows her to fill in for any team member whenever an extra link is needed to see a task through to its conclusion. Her pleasant personality, independent thinking, and fair approach to dealing with people would endear her to the team and persuade them to respect and trust her.

Self-effacing
Some people may need to be persuaded to put themselves forward.

Promotion • 2

Priorities
*When considering a promotion,
think carefully about the consequences
for your personal life.*

Some of us think we are ready
for a promotion when we are not.
Perhaps we have had insufficient
preparation or are not fully aware of
what advancement will mean in the
way of responsibility and stress. We
may be too busy thinking of being able
to move to a larger house, take a more
exotic vacation, or fulfill a dream.
Instead, we need to think about how
our lives will change because of the
promotion, both in the work
environment, as well as with our friends
and families. A promotion usually involves

taking on more responsibility and may
involve travel, moving to an unfamiliar
area, or seeing less of your family.

Common qualities

For a successful promotion, the
individual will benefit from possessing
healthy self-esteem, being flexible, and
having an ability to mediate in an
articulate and practical way. Empathy is
also often a useful attribute. For the
higher levels of a promotion, more than
management skills will be necessary.
There are some characteristics that are
always welcome at any level. Being
articulate, polite, and using common
sense, along with taking responsibility,
making decisions, and sorting out
problems are all beneficial qualities.

Sometimes a promotion can mean a
new career rather than just a step up
the ladder. For example, an educational
art professional may leave the school
where she has been working and join
a company as the leader of a design
team. On the other hand, a creative
mathematics teacher wanting a change

and promotion may leave the school environment and join the internet revolution as a web designer.

There are so many different opportunities for a promotion, whether you stay in the same organization, move elsewhere, or take up a completely new career. The important factor is for you to be flexible, aware of your own personality characteristics, and ready to learn new skills.

Sometimes a promotion can mean leaving the security of a company and branching out on your own as an independent consultant or freelancer`. In order to succeed in such a venture, it is vital to possess the qualities that are needed to work on your own. If you do not have these qualities and feel that you cannot learn them, you will need to find a business partner whose talents will complement yours.

If you are considering a promotion or setting up your own business, it can be useful to ask close friends and family to provide you with their assessment of your strengths and weaknesses.

Supporting roles
The workers in this dentist's office need to work alongside each other to achieve their goals.

TEAMWORK • 1

The people who provided these three samples work together as a team: a dentist, a dental nurse, and a receptionist. They work side by side in a busy dentist's office. This makes them an ideal example of the uses to which handwriting analysis can be put when it comes to analyzing and organizing teams.

The Receptionist

• Her gentle left slant shows loyalty

• The mixture of some letters being connected while others are disjoined, plus her garland letter forms, show that she is adaptable and good with people

• The small size of her writing, which is fairly simplified and rounded, shows that she can be practical and can deal with people speedily, yet pleasantly

The Dental Nurse

• Her right slant, narrowness, and some angles show that she is empathetic but single-minded; she will give her full attention to the task at hand

• Clear word and line spacing show that she is able to think ahead, plan, and organize things to ensure that the working day runs as smoothly as possible

The Dentist

• His fairly upright slant, thin stroke, and narrowness reflect his desire to give the whole of his energy to his job

• His fairly wide word spacing indicates that he likes to work on a one-to-one basis, which is ideal in his profession

• The thin stroke of the pen shows his analytical mind

• The uprightness of the letters shows that he is able to stick to known methodology in his execution of treatment

Love gives naught but itself and takes
naught but from itself. Love possesses
not nor would be possessed; for love
is sufficient unto love.

Kahlil Gibran.

THE RECEPTIONIST

Kindness is more important than
wisdom, and the recognition of
this is the beginning of wisdom.

Theodore Isaac Rubin

THE DENTAL NURSE

All great deeds and all great thoughts
have a ridiculous beginning. Great works
are often born on a street corner
or in a restaurant's revolving door.

Albert Camus.

THE DENTIST

Teamwork • 2

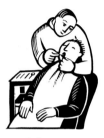

Safety net
When performing delicate tasks like dentistry, it is essential to know that you are backed up by your work team.

Winning teams have to be created. Once established, successful teams need maintaining, nurturing, and developing. Building mutual confidence and trust among any group of people working together is essential.

For most of us, belonging to various groups is an everyday part of life. We may hold different positions within a range of organizations, and we choose to exercise our various strengths in order to adapt and fit in with each particular group. Effective teams consist of people with different skills working in harmony together, pooling their knowledge and talents positively for the benefit of the whole group, and for any customers or clients that rely on the group. In most groups, it is productive to have a leader, an ideas person, a practical individual, someone who will be able to look at both sides of any discussion, and a mediator. All team members need to know what goal has been decided, a plan of action to reach the target, and what each person is expected to do and achieve. Regular communication, updates, feedback, and changes of plan and priorities are also important factors in creating a successful group.

Stages to winning

There are several stages to developing a winning team. First, there will be a testing of the rules to see what is essential and what is not needed. At the second stage, there is usually some group conflict; one or more people will cause friction and disharmony. Only when this has been worked through and overcome can true bonding develop, allowing the team to accept one another, and support each other.

Once the group has been formed, it will need maintenance. Individual requirements will have to be met within the group. Incentives and natural competition with another group can also be useful ways to keep the team motivated and working together. Training, loyalty, communication, support, encouragement—and each person pulling their own weight—are also essential factors that make a group successful. Flexibility and learning to understand the talents of other members of the team can help the group to grow and develop. If someone becomes ill or has to go away for a short time, then other members will be able to share the workload and keep the task on course.

Winning teams boost the self-esteem of all members and create harmony. This leads to a better performance, increased motivation, and the self-discipline to keep going.

Experience required

Special abilities are needed for unusual and unfamiliar working environments and projects.

RECRUITMENT • 1

The following unusual task needed a leader. The first part of the assignment was to organize a team, then lead, and drive them in a truck with equipment to help some refugees in Eastern Europe. The second part of the job was to help construct whatever the most urgent task was deemed to be once the truck arrived at its destination. The sample shows the leader chosen.

> It's easier to get forgiv
> it is to get permission
> think it's right, do it. If i
> you will be praised. If it
> you can always apologi

Compassionate Leader

The right slant and broadness of his writing indicate an empathetic person with the drive to keep going, however tough the challenges. The connected letters, combined with an original style, show that he has creative ideas that he can evaluate logically. Although his line spacing is close, there is dovetailing, reflecting his ability to think quickly. There is some roundedness in the letter forms, along with close word spacing, which means that he enjoys being with people. With the irregularity and broad width in his writing, he is flexible and willing to fit in with the team, changing priorities as and when new situations arise.

Strong drive

Logical thinking

Responsibility
This position requires skills of leadership, analysis, and empathy.

Recruitment • 2

First impressions
The face-to-face interview is just one way to assess whether a candidate has the right skills.

Finding the right person to fit a job description can be challenging. In this world of ever-changing requirements, one may start an assignment with the necessary qualities, but as time goes on, one may need to acquire additional skills for new tasks.

Wise planning and forethought are essential. If a person is being recruited to replace an individual who is leaving, it is worthwhile spending time with the departing employee to find out exactly what their role is and how a replacement would best fill that role.

It is also beneficial for the immediate superior of the position to be updated on what tasks and skills are best needed to fill this post.

Personality

Having decided on the skills needed for the position, the next item on the agenda is to consider the personality of the new employee. For some jobs, a pleasant personality and the ability to get along with everyone is more important than brilliance in one skill. At other times, professional expertise will be the first consideration.

In the creative world of advertising, the ability to have original thoughts and new ideas may be the most important factor when potential staff are considered. If a candidate seems likely to bring in a lot of new business but is prone to bursts of bad temper, it may be worth offering him a short-term contract. At the end of the contract, the quantity of business that has been acquired can be weighed up against the difficulties of the employee's personality.

Looking at the handwriting of prospective employees will allow the analyst to gauge the personalities of the people applying for the post. It can also indicate how each candidate will fit in with the rest of the team.

There are some jobs where it is extremely difficult to find a person with all the skills and personality traits required. Often people who have exceptional talent in the sales field have difficulty completing paperwork. This situation may be resolved by a creative yet firm assistant who can regularly extricate the information required to fill in all the routine, but necessary, documents. They could work as a team and, in this case, it would be vital for the salesperson to respect and work with the assistant positively, thus ensuring that all sales are handled and completed thoroughly and on time. With the right partnership in place (mutual respect will always be required), this pair could form a successful team, and bring a lot of new business to the company.

Back on track

Many women are nervous when they return to their workplace after their children start to attend school.

RECRUITMENT • 3
This writer has applied for a job as a general assistant in an office. She has been out of the work scene for ten years while she was bringing up her children. They are now all at school and she is a little anxious about returning to work. This writer may be nervous in an interview situation, because she feels out of touch with the workplace. An analysis of her handwriting reveals clear line spacing, which shows that she can plan and organize her time.

Wide word spacing

Slightly mixed slant

Connected letters

Connected letters

> Hilflos. suchte ich in meinen Taschen nach Zigaretten, obwohl ich wusste, dass ich keine mehr hatte. wohl noch eine Packung im Auto lag, aber das Auto stand zwanzig Meter rechts von der Haustür, und etwas wie ein Ozean lag zwischen mir und dem Auto.

Logical

The wide word spacing and left slant show that this woman can work on her own. The connectedness in her writing means that she enjoys a logical approach to her work. There is also some regularity in her writing, which shows that she likes to follow a routine.

Reliable

Analysis of this woman's handwriting shows her to be logical and dependable.

Recruitment • 4

Times change
*Some skills, such as filing, are
becoming increasingly obsolete
as technology changes.*

There are some jobs whose
specification remains the same for
many years. When change does
come, a lot of employee training may
be needed and staff who have been
with the organization for a long time
may leave for various reasons having
to do with the new innovations.

Knowing where documents can be
located will always be necessary in an
organization. Filing clerks, whose task
it is to file important documents, used
to have an assured job. With the
introduction of computers, there is still
a need for some paperwork to be kept

safely locked away. However, more
and more files are being kept on
computer disks. Filing clerks may now
have to learn to type and use the
computer. For those who enjoy routine,
change can bring fear. New
technology may mean jobs will become
obsolete. Reassurances to staff members
that plenty of work and sufficient
training will be given are therefore a
wise precaution.

Preparation for recruiting new people
to do routine work still needs careful
planning. While some people enjoy
routine, the safety of knowing exactly
what is expected of them, and what
their job entails, they can also be
trained to learn new technology that
will give them the same safety and
routine as they had before.

Happy employees

It is important to keep staff members
fully informed at all stages regarding
changes in the workplace. Some
people will leave and this may mean
that you will have to recruit a new

group of people. They may be working in the same department, so it is worthwhile taking time to recruit a team of people who not only have the skills required, but are also able to cooperate and work together. This will pay dividends in the long run; happy staff will stay and help each other through the various crises that occur from time to time in any organization.

A highly creative person who interviews people for a safe, routine job may have difficulty selecting the right individuals. This is where handwriting analysis is a tremendous asset. It shows the qualities present in each candidate and gives the interviewer concrete and objective information.

Many of us highlight our best qualities when we are interviewed for a new job. Interviewers are also human and may be attracted to certain personalities, whether they have the relevant requirements or not. The handwriting analyst doesn't usually see the candidates and so can be completely objective in her analysis of applicants.

Fitting together
New enterprises will always require people with complementary sets of skills.

BUSINESS COMPATIBILITY • 1 James

and Angela are thinking about setting up a business together to sell various types of gadgets. A sample analysis of their handwriting helps to reveal the ways in which their personality traits will contribute to the success—or otherwise—of the venture. It also indicates that they both have different strengths that may blend well together.

Marked right slant

Large lower zone

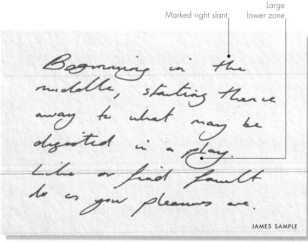

JAMES SAMPLE

Rules are made for the obedience of fools and The guidance of wise men.

chinese Proverb.

ANGELA SAMPLE

Stable baseline   Upright slant

Flamboyant

James's writing has a marked rightward slant, which means that he will enjoy the challenge of sales. The fact that some of his lines dovetail means that he likes to think on his feet, which is an important asset in a selling situation. However, one of his weaknesses is that he will always try to avoid doing paperwork. The irregular baselines in his handwriting are a sign that he will flourish at being creative and using his initiative in a professional situation; he loves variety and change. To him, filling in forms is boring and he may have difficulty in this area.

Stable

Angela, whose handwriting includes an upright slant and some use of garlands, will enjoy handling the customer-relationship side of the business. With her clear line spacing and fairly regular writing, she is obviously well suited to dealing with complex office paperwork. Her clear layout indicates she is good at planning her time and at organizing, and her straight baselines indicate that she is the more stable character of the pair. Angela will be able to handle the day-to-day routine, possibly monotonous, work that is required to keep a successful business going.

Business Compatibility • 2

Friendship and compatibility
While amicable relationships are important in the workplace, professional skills should also be considered.

For a successful business partnership, it is important for partners to possess, between them, the various different strengths needed to cover all of the requirements that are necessary in order for a business to thrive and prosper.

Friends sometimes decide to go into business together. Often their friendship is based on a number of common personality traits. While this may enhance friendship, it could ruin a business partnership if some vital skills are missing. Differences in personality types can be both positive and negative. On the positive side, acknowledgment and acceptance can blend the partnership, but, on the negative side, it can introduce a blame culture.

Experts required

In general, most businesses need expertise in the following areas: selling, accounting, planning, marketing, training, advertising, customer relations, research, and development. If a team can pull together, communicate, be flexible, learn new skills, update their existing knowledge, change priorities when necessary, and remain cool in a crisis, this will be a great asset.

Business partnerships that can incorporate all of the above skills and personality traits have a good chance of succeeding.

There are many other factors, such as market research, commitment, and finance that need to be sorted out while the business plan is being put together. At the ideas stage, partners need to develop the ability to research productively, listen attentively, make changes positively, and continue to learn in as many useful areas as possible. A great asset is someone's ability to hear professional advice, and then look objectively at what has been suggested.

Success comes not only through hard work, but also by being prepared for the business and approaching it in an appropriate manner. People need to communicate, discuss, and compromise all the time. Sorting out difficulties as they arise is a major factor in reaching successful targets.

Positive attributes can easily be recognized and put to use. Looking at negatives can be a tricky business. Once we have accepted our own weaknesses, we can then choose whether to do something about them, or just accept that those are areas where we will always need help. When you and your partners have all been through this process and can accept each other's shortcomings, you have a solid foundation on which you will be able to expand your business.

THE EMOTIONS

Handwriting analysis can play a useful role in assisting individuals to recognize some of their own emotions as well as those of their friends, family, and colleagues at work. Some of us like to let everyone know how we are feeling; others prefer to keep their feelings to themselves. We all experience the entire range of emotions, but we may not be aware of them, or choose to put them on display. ✑ Sometimes, however, we say or do something that is totally out of character. This can happen when we have very strong feelings about something and words can be expressed in haste in what may be an inappropriate form. Becoming aware of our emotions gives us the chance to learn what we feel, and perhaps even become aware of its origins.

Introduction to Emotions

Powerful feelings
*Both pressure and slant yield clues
as to whether you are passionate
or self-controlled.*

We all have emotions, although some may try to deny it! Some people say that they are never angry and they may never actively yell or lose their temper at other people; however, their anger will show in other ways. Silence and the refusal to comply with a loved one's wishes is a passive display of anger.

Love is a word with many meanings and probably just as many different ways of being displayed. Some individuals wear their hearts on their sleeves and fall in and out of love easily. The passion of the moment may be intense, and yet these people appear to recover remarkably quickly when they fall out of love.

There are others who have strong feelings but may not express their love in words; for them, love is a totally absorbing feeling. The end of a love affair can be traumatic for these individuals, and may even cause them to sink into depression or another illness while coming to terms with the situation.

Emotional intensity

The amount of pressure that we produce in handwriting is a reflection of the depth of our feelings. The stronger the indentation into the paper, the more intense our feelings. The slant in our writing is an indicator of how we show our emotions.

In a handwriting sample, the right slant tends to indicate someone who wears his heart on his sleeve, but this is not always the case. When the rhythm is rigid, such a writer will exert self-control to keep his feelings to himself.

Occasionally, when the strength of feelings becomes too strong, there will be a verbal explosion as he is forced to openly express himself.

People who write with a leftward slant tend to keep their feelings to themselves. Their feelings may be just as deep as those with a right slant, but, for them, inner reflection takes the place of outer display.

The more that someone's handwriting slopes to the left or to the right, the more intensely the writer is aware of his or her emotions, while individuals whose handwriting displays an upright slant will usually have a more balanced approach to self-expression. It is relatively rare for writers with an upright writing slant to be very passionate. They can fall in love and will have deep feelings, but they will not know the intensity of emotion that is felt by writers with strongly sloping handwriting. For the upright writer, wise thoughts, plans, and actions are more important than impulsive, spontaneous bursts of emotions.

EMOTIONAL ANALYSIS

To assess a person's emotions by their handwriting, it is essential to find at least three different writing movements with the same interpretation. Let us take the right slant, which usually denotes a warm, kind, easygoing, and extrovert personality—someone who wears her heart on her sleeve. In order for this interpretation to be correct, other movements, such as close word spacing, garland letter forms, and broad width would need to be present. If, instead of the above movements, the right slant is accompanied by a rigid rhythm and wide word spacing, the writer could be a shy person and quite withdrawn.

Wide word space

Left slant

Only that day dawns
to which we are awake
There is more day to dawn
The sun is but a morning
star

Thoreau

AVOIDING INTENSITY SAMPLE

Avoiding Intensity

This sample shows a fairly upright slant, which indicates that the writer avoids showing intense emotions. Her ability to think on her feet and her practical approach to life mean that she is philosophical rather than dramatic.

Passionate

This writer has a marked right slant, indicating that he has strong emotions. There is a certain rigidity in the rhythm, which shows that he would like to exercise control over his feelings. His passionate feelings may sometimes be overwhelming, but he is a warm, enthusiastic person.

Rigid rhythm

Connected

Friends are not only together when they are side-by-side. Even one who is far away…. is still in our thoughts

Ludwig von Beethoven

PASSIONATE SAMPLE

Sharing Emotions

The general style of this sample and the spontaneous irregularity of the middle zone show that this writer likes to share her emotion with others. This helps her to come to terms with a situation in which she is upset, and enhances her happiness when she has had a good experience and wants to share it with others.

Rigid rhythm

"Similemente agli splendor mondani; Ordinò general ministra e duca, Che permutasse a tempo li ben vani, Di gente in gente, e, d'uno in altro sangue.
Inf. VII 77

SHARING EMOTIONS SAMPLE

Relationships •1

Compromise is vital
Without give and take, it would be difficult for any relationship to survive.

There are many different types of relationship. Some are in the workplace, and require individuals to have good working relationships with their colleagues. Others are with our families and friends, or may spark up through mutual attraction.

When two people experience love at first sight, they will see only the positive characteristics of their new-found partner. Their feelings of love will cloud any objectivity where weak personality traits are concerned. But once this phase has passed, then one

or both of the individuals will begin to see the flaws in their partner's personality. At this stage, some couples break up and decide to end their relationship. For couples to develop a lasting and happy relationship, it is important for both to accept the weaknesses in each other. When this happens, the relationship has laid one of the foundation stones to a long-lasting and rewarding time together. Other assets for developing a happy and fulfilling long-term relationship are a warm and friendly approach, treating each other as equals, and working out a smooth and easy way to interact.

Relationship basics

Giving full attention, showing a keen and, if needed, sympathetic interest in each other, and communicating on the same wavelength are also vital foundation stones. Minor misunderstandings can turn into huge problems if they are not recognized and handled as they arise. Building trust, giving commitment, and determining boundaries all take time, patience, and discussion. The powerful emotion of love can so easily cloud fundamental differences in personalities that a long-lasting relationship may not be sustainable after the first flush of love has ebbed away.

If you are not in a relationship now, it could be wise to decide what you are really looking for in an ideal partner— not just personality characteristics, but way of life, attitudes, and all the other things that go together to make a good relationship. Knowing what you want is one thing, but, inevitably, compromise will be necessary. While you are level-headed, it is easier to think rationally about what is essential for your life, and what is adaptable and may be yielded.

Handwriting analysis may be used to help couples look at their relationships. Analysis can indicate compatibility in personality characteristics, and identify areas that will cause friction. A analyst can give an objective appraisal and suggest areas where compromise will need to be discussed.

RELATIONSHIPS • 2

This couple wanted to have their handwriting analyzed so that they could learn more about one another, and about the dynamics of their relationship. Some of the analyst's interpretations referred to character traits that the couple were already aware of, but others came as a surprise to one or both of them.

> The years between fifty + Seventy
> are the hardest. You are
> always being asked to do
> things, and yet you are
> not decrepit enough to
> turn them down.
> T. S. Eliot

RACHEL

Rounded letter form

Large middle zone

Characters revealed
How well do you know your partner? A handwriting analysis could surprise both of you.

Small middle zone

> When you have work to do
> and you don't want to do it,
> decide what really needs to be
> done and what can wait.
> Unknown.

Wavy line form

DAVID

Looking at the writing of the two people in these samples, they are well suited in many areas. Rachel's writing sample shows a large middle zone, which complements the small middle zone indicated in David's writing. This means that Rachel is happy to talk while David is content to listen. However, Rachel is also a good listener, and David enjoys an in-depth discussion from time to time, preferably with one other person. What makes this relationship particularly rewarding is that both partners share fundamental personality traits, such as being communicative, supporting each other, giving encouragement, being flexible, and having a good sense of humor.

LETTER FORMS
David's letter forms are a mixture of angular and wavy lines, which shows that he has determination. This shows that he can also be flexible, which fits in with Rachel's rounded letter forms, which show she is a naturally friendly person.

ZONES
David has a dominant upper zone, indicating his thoughts and ideas for the future, while Rachel has a dominant middle zone, which means she is practical and gets on with life.

LINE SPACING
Both have clear line spacing, showing that planning and organizing come naturally.

Relationships • 3

Middle-age changes
Carl Jung believed that dormant emotions and feelings can surface as a person grows older.

There are many different types of relationships and many reasons why two people choose to share their lives together. Sometimes people with totally opposite characteristics can enjoy a good partnership, while other couples who have little in common do nothing but argue and criticize. Where two individuals have many very opposite personality traits, a lot of tolerance and acceptance by both parties is necessary. Sometimes people will stay together for many years and then decide to live separate lives.

According to Carl Jung (1875–1961), we all have four functions: thinking, feeling, sensing, and intuition. These four functions work in two pairs. If thinking is a person's primary function, then its opposite pair, feeling, will be their fourth function, and therefore in the unconscious.

Jung believed that when we reach middle age, the fourth function, which has lain dormant in the unconscious, may start to develop. It may cause different reactions, attitudes, and behaviors in individuals. People who have been pure thinkers all their lives, using facts and logic to make decisions, may start to think about their feelings and emotions. For their partners, who may not yet have started to develop their own fourth function, this change may come as a welcome relief, or it may have the opposite effect.

It is at this time that couples have the opportunity either to become closer, or to move further apart from one another and suffer more misunderstandings. They may move away from each other, thus causing further anger, friction, or resentment, and perhaps leading to a permanent end of the long-term liaison.

Successful couples

Couples who have always communicated well and supported each other through the trials and tribulations of life, as well as the exciting and successful times, will usually handle these personality changes more easily and constructively than relationships where there has not been a lot of rapport and flexibility between people. These changes can enhance the relationship once both partners recognize, accept, and talk through what is going on and, if necessary, agree new boundaries and different ways of doing things while still being loving and supportive of each other.

Just because two people are different from each other does not mean they must separate in order to be happy. The most important aspects of a good relationship are mutual respect and understanding, and love.

RELATIONSHIPS • 4

In the samples of writing on this page, the couple have very different personalities and have obviously worked out how to enjoy a relationship that suits their various needs. Mary may well have been drawn to John for his love of adventure and travel. She will be happy to let him plan their outings and, given her flexibility, she will cope well with sudden changes in the schedule should they occur.

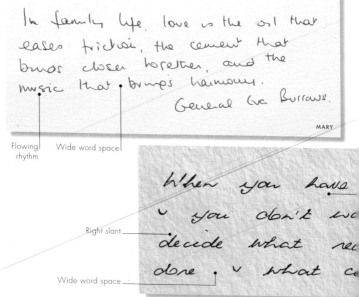

In family life, love is the oil that eases friction, the cement that binds closer together, and the music that brings harmony.

General Eva Burrows.

MARY

Flowing rhythm

Wide word space

Right slant

Wide word space

When you have you don't wa decide what rea done, what c

Different Strokes

SLANTS
Although their writing slants in different directions, his right slant and rigidity are the way John shows his passion.

LETTER FORMS AND RHYTHM
Mary's rounded letter forms and rhythmic flow show that she is more easygoing than John is, which acts as a calming influence on him.

WORD SPACING
Both John and Mary have wide word spacing and will enjoy spending time on their own. They may well have separate interests and friends, and go in different directions during the day, then share the day's events in the evening.

Opposites
If one partner is adaptable, there is a good chance that the relationship will be successful.

Rigidity

work to do
to do it,
needs to be
wait.

JOHN

Personal Development •1

Peak condition
*Personal development complements
other kinds of conditioning, such as
regular physical exercise.*

Personal development is an area
from which we can all benefit
should we choose to do so. As
our life progresses, we will find that
we may start to question the thought
processes or behavior patterns we have
always followed, and with which we
are familiar. We will find that we are
not always happy to accept a situation
or theory just because it has been this
way for a long time.

When we gradually start to question
these responses, we will also begin to
recognize that there is an actual desire

for change starting to take place within
us. The more we are able to accept that
we are on the path to self-development
and personal growth, the more likely
we will be able to succeed with future
changes. We must always remember
that the need and desire for change
must exist first before new methods,
ways, and attitudes can succeed.

Discipline
A lot of hard work and self-discipline
will be needed to shift the beliefs and
habits of a lifetime if we are to take the
first tentative steps of change. The
physical side of our development is one
of the first disciplines to consider. Getting
regular exercise—such as walking or
playing golf—and developing mental
concentration also help us to experience
the emotional rewards to be gained by
changing or developing our interests.
As we become fitter through regular
exercise regimes, so our level of self-
esteem will also increase so that we
can start to set ourselves small physical
goals that are achievable.

It is important to recognize that we all have strengths. However, it is also essential for us to accept that, likewise, we all have weaknesses. Depending on the degree of our perceived imperfections, it can sometimes be profitable to consult an expert. Often you will have an idea as to what sort of help you would like. It is important to remember that the expert you choose is only there to assist you in your development and is not someone on whom to rely or who can solve all the problems that may be present in your life. Sometimes it is easy to become unwittingly dependent on the person who is helping you. Short term, this may be useful, but, long term, it is vital to regain your independence in a way that will help you keep your own counsel and progress alone.

Determination to Succeed

This is indicated by medium–heavy pressure, a mixture of angle and garland letter forms, broad width, rising baselines, and clear word and line spacing.

PERSONAL DEVELOPMENT • 2

Being objective about oneself can be an enlightening experience. The existence of certain personality characteristics that have been pointed out by friends or professionals needs to be reflected upon in the most open-minded and objective way possible. This can be rewarding for somebody asking advice about personal growth, but it may take time to come to terms with the information. You have to scrutinize your personality carefully and in depth. The writer of this sample has decided that she would like to make changes. It is a good idea to see what sort of energy she has and how she uses it now. Once areas for possible change have been identified, she can then begin to work on one feature at a time.

Large middle zone

Horizontal mingling

When you're sad, think about what would be comforting When you're hurt, Tell the Person who hurt you. Keeping it inside makes it grow unknown.

PRESSURE
The writer puts her vitality into being practical and enjoying the company of other people. This can be deduced from the firm pressure she uses and her dominant middle zone.

BROADNESS
With the broadness in her writing, this writer likes to hear fresh ideas and is keen to try out new ventures, as long as they are of fairly short duration.

AREAS FOR CHANGE
There are several areas where she could benefit from looking at change. One possibility is to enjoy more of her own company; another is to develop and plan some long-term ambitions. She would probably feel happier working with someone else; she would appreciate the support and encouragement which, in turn, could speed up her achievements regarding change.

Keep an open mind
When you analyze your own handwriting, you will need to be as objective as possible.

Personal Development • 3

Accept the challenge
*Believe in your own ability
to improve, and your capacity
to learn more about yourself.*

This is where handwriting analysis can be a helpful tool. By determining the type of personality someone has as well as behavior and attitude, a handwriting analyst can aid a therapist in determining the best way to work with a client so that progress can be made. There are handwriting exercises that can be given to a client but, in order for them to work, the client needs to focus on an area of her personality that she would like to change first. The exercises can then be tailored accordingly.

Personal development really is your unique, individual way of becoming more aware and adjusted to your life structure. Some people may find that they become obsessed with themselves as they consider their future, while, for others, avoidance of core issues is a natural option. There is no right or wrong way that can easily be learned; we are all on our own unique paths to the future. Finding a satisfying path involves trial and error.

Different methods

For some people, the gentle approach may be vital. Other individuals may prefer to work on practical and mechanical exercises. With so many methods on offer, a mixture of different techniques may be the best way forward in some cases. Personal development is about constantly learning, gaining information about ourselves, and having the confidence to expand on the knowledge, as well as exercising discipline.

As challenges are presented to us, we may find that we can act with empathy and acceptance. At other times, we may have to brace ourselves and use all the self-discipline we possess to overcome an obstacle. It is a question of meeting each challenge as it happens and dealing with it in a way that makes us feel comfortable and inspires us with confidence.

It is exciting to think that there are many ways in which we can help ourselves to develop. Although, at some stage, professional expertise may be useful, there is so much more that we can achieve for ourselves once we have built our confidence levels up to the stage where we can believe in our own individual abilities.

If you decide that, initially, you would like to seek professional help, there are plenty of books that name hundreds of organizations of this nature. When you find a system that appeals to you, make sure that the individual expert you choose is also the sort of person who will suit your needs.

PERSONAL DEVELOPMENT • 4

It is one thing for an expert to have all the qualifications that are required; however, if you find that you cannot quite relate to their personality, then it is sensible to keep searching for one who has the wisdom, empathy, kindness, and flexibility you require to take that vital step forward. Make sure that the expert you choose is also a person with whom you can feel completely relaxed and confident, and that you trust, so that you are both working toward the shared goal of your personal growth.

Clear word space   Arrhythmic   Very connected

> Dann! waren welche an d
> Wir sähen das Licht, "s
> sie, „ vom Fenster. Wir
> uns zehn Minuten hins

This writer would benefit from professional expertise in the fields of yoga, meditation, aromatherapy, or reflexology—all treatments that would help to relax her and make her feel more at ease. When she chooses an expert in complementary therapies, it will be vital that she feels a rapport with and a sense of trust in her teacher. This will enable her to feel comfortable during the treatments, which in turn will mean that she will be able to restore her balance and harmony.

WELL ORGANIZED

The writer of this sample uses a light pressure, and has connected letters, arrhythmic writing, and quite clear word and line spacing. This indicates that she plans and organizes well and so makes the best possible use of her available energy.

VARIETY

The writing overall is irregular, reflecting the enjoyment she derives from having lots of variety in her life. The connected letters indicate that she takes a logical approach to life. She would benefit from allowing intuitive thoughts to prevail over pure logic for some of the time.

Tür,,,
zten
vollera
zen.

Relaxation
There are many different ways to relax, from yoga to tap dancing.

Personal Development • 5

Become fulfilled
*Positive change for personal
development can take place
at any point in your life.*

means that this was not the best time
for this information to have been given
to you. At a later stage in your life, you
may be given the same information
again, and this time you will be ready
to act on it, because it has become
crucial to your further development.
When something like this happens, not
only is it an interesting learning stage in
your development, but it also should
prove to you that you are on the right
path toward personal growth.

Personal growth is a long and slow
process. Anything achieved quickly
may be superficial. Sometimes
pieces of information slot into place
within a short time. However, it often
takes years for simple, yet profound,
advice to filter through to the
unconscious and allow positive change
to take place.

This is where timing can prove
essential. You may be given a piece of
information at a certain stage in your
life, but, for one reason or another,
choose not to follow it up. This usually

Never too old

One of the most exciting and rewarding
aspects of personal growth and
development is that we are never too
old to change. Personal development
may start at any age and may also be
a lifelong pursuit. There are always
plenty of ways to learn and absorb,
and room to develop.

There are people who have written a
first book at the age of 80 or more and
become famous. What we need to
change and develop ourselves is the
drive, the motivation, the discipline,

and the excitement of becoming a more fulfilled person. Perfection is not the ultimate goal in personal growth; there is no such thing as the perfect human being. However, acquiring wisdom, acting with love in a kind, genuine, and giving way toward others and ourselves can keep us striving to achieve our goals, especially in our more challenging moments.

Some people have their own image of how they would like to be, while others prefer to admire someone else's characteristics. Mother Teresa of Calcutta—whose only possessions on death were two saris and a bucket— is an example of someone who has inspired many people to challenge their own behavior and assumptions. Someone like this could be an inspiration to you; however, you might admire the qualities and character of a completely different sort of public personality. The function of having such an inspirational figure in the background is to have a helpful aid on your own path of self-discovery.

HANDWRITING EXERCISES • 1

Through personal development, we are looking for the best way to achieve balance and harmony. There are many physical actions that are calming and refreshing for the mind, such as physical exercise or deep breathing. Handwriting analysis can help with the recognition and elimination of characteristics from the personality by changing features of handwriting.

Suspended downstroke 1

Suspended downstroke 2

Suspended downstroke 3

People can be very peculiar. They are often driven by their deep-seated emotions without realising it. This produces a range of responses we call human.

Anon.

Great Potential

BECOMING INDEPENDENT
In this sample, the writer has a dominant middle zone and close word spacing, indicating that she thrives on being with people. For her, learning to enjoy time alone will bring great rewards and real independence.

GROWING SELF-CONFIDENCE
Look at the way the lower case letter "n" is formed. The second downstroke is slightly suspended in the air and does not quite reach the baseline. This shows us that her inhibitions stop her from achieving great things. If she could consciously make an effort when writing to ensure that the downstroke reaches the baseline, this will help her to realize her self-confidence, which in turn will be an asset to achieving her goals.

Changes
You can eliminate unwanted character traits by changing aspects of your handwriting.

Handwriting Exercises • 2

Be determined

Changing movements in your handwriting will have little effect unless you concentrate.

Handwriting exercises can be used to change aspects of the personality. For these to work, however, someone must actively want to achieve a different attitude or behavior. Aimless practicing, whatever the goal, is wasted unless the person has a purpose and a plan for implementing change. It is necessary for the analyst to find out from the client the purpose of her desire to change, and to ascertain through analyzing her handwriting how much discipline she has.

It is vital to carry out only one exercise at a time. Altering fundamental characteristics of the personality that have been present for most of a person's life is going to take time and, when successful, will inevitably have some far-reaching repercussions. The writer may lose some old friends, take up a completely new career, or go traveling. The possibilities are boundless and various.

If someone has a family with which he lives, it may be useful to have a chat with his partner. Sometimes the partner may be the source of the problem; in such cases it will be wiser to seek support and advice from someone else known to the writer. Friends can be helpful, but they may have difficulty understanding the changes in their friend. This may cause friction. When she has assessed the client's situation, the graphotherapist may be able to suggest suitable types of support. The client needs to be made aware of the reverberating effects that change can have and the transformations that could take place. It is wise to look at all aspects of a situation, even if some are difficult to imagine.

The perfect balance

It is prudent to remember that there is no perfect writing style. Balance is seen in the writing of a person who has achieved inner harmony. Graphotherapy exercises are aimed at helping someone achieve a feeling of inner contentment. We all have our own agenda, and happiness is unique to each of us. A perceptive analyst will assist a client individually when choosing a course of action.

The handwriting analyst, by analyzing the writing of her client, can point out his strengths and then look at areas in his personality and life that are ripe for possible improvement. The client will probably be able to accept that he has certain weaknesses and may have a list of one or more characteristics that he is aware he needs to change.

None of us will ever be perfect, and so it is vital that we choose to work on aspects of our character that can actually be changed and that will bring us a measure of contentment when we achieve the transition.

FURTHER READING

AMEND, KAREN and RUIZ, MARY, *Handwriting Analysis.*

BARON, RENEE and WAGELE, ELIZABETH, *The Enneagram Made Easy.*

CURRER-BIGGS, NOEL, *Handwriting Analysis in Business: The Use of Handwriting analysis in the Personnel Section.*

DAWSON, MICHAEL, *Healing the Cause.*

EVERARD, BERTIE and MORRIS, GEOFFREY, *Effective School Management.*

HARRISON, PHYLLIS, *Helping Your Health Through Handwriting.*

HARTFORD, HUNTINGDON, *You Are What You Write.*

HILL, BARABARA, *Handwriting analysis.*

HOLDER, ROBERT, *You Can Analyze Handwriting.*

KURDSEN, STEPHEN, *Reading Character From Handwriting.*

LEIBEL, *Change your Handwriting, Change your Life.*

MCGRAW, DR. PHILLIP C, *Life Strategies.*

MENDEL, ALFRED O, *Personality in Handwriting.*

RUSKAN, JOHN, *Emotional Clearing.*

SAUDEK, ROBERT, *Experiments with Handwriting.*

SAUDEK, ROBERT, *The Psychology of Handwriting.*

SINGER, ERIC, *Personality in Handwriting.*

TEW, JACQUI, *Handwriting.*

WEST, PETER, *Handwriting analysis: Understanding What Handwriting Means.*

USEFUL ADDRESSES

American Association of Handwriting
Analysts
PO Box 95, Southfield
Michigan, 48037-0095
Tel: 248 262 4850
Fax: 248 262 4851
Email: AAHAOffice@aol.com
Website: www.handwriting.org/aaha

International School of
Handwriting Sciences
498 Corbett Avenue
San Francisco, CA 94114
Tel: 415 864 3332
Email: twidmer@flash.net
Website:
www.handwriting.org/ishs/index.html

International Graphoanalysis Society
111N Canal Street, Chicago
Illinois, 60606
Tel: 312 930 9446
Fax: 312 930 5903
Email: headquarters@igas.com
Website: www.igas.com

National Society of Graphology
250 West 57th Street, Suite 2032
New York, 10107
Tel: 212 265 1148
Fax: 212 307 5671
Email: Rogwrite@aol.com

Glossary

Absolute size The measurement from the top of letters such as "b" and "h" to the bottom of letters such as "g" and "y."

Angle A letter form whereby the two downstrokes of the lower case "n" meet to make a point at the top of the middle zone.

Arcade A letter form whereby the two downstrokes of the lower case "n" are joined at the top in a rounded movement.

Arrhythm Disjointed and jerky writing movements.

Baseline The imaginary line upon which you write.

Connected When three or four letters in each word are joined together.

Copybook The handwriting style taught to the writer as a child.

Disconnected When most letters are not joined up.

Dominant movements Those handwriting movements that occur every time the pen touches the paper, for example spacing and pressure.

Dovetail The descenders from the line above that fit into the space on the line below without touching the ascenders in that line.

Enriched A type of style whereby extra loops are added to the essential writing.

Garland A rounded letter form.

Horizontal mingling This occurs when the middle zone letters touch each other without a connecting stroke.

Letter forms The formation of individual letters: e.g., angle, arcade, and garland.

Line spacing The space that can be seen between the lines.

Mingling lines This occurs when the descenders from the line above are intertwined with the ascenders of the line below.

Miscellaneous movements Those movements which occur from time to time, for example the "i" dot and the "t" cross.

Neglected When essential downstrokes are missing from the letter forms.

Pasty A thick pen stroke.

Pen thickness A thick or a thin stroke, depending on the choice of pen.

Pressure The indentation on a piece of paper caused by handwriting pressure.

Primary thread A mix of three or more different letter forms.

Regularity The amount of regularity present in writing movements.

Relative size The measure or size of any one zone.

Rhythm The flow of the writing movement.

Secondary thread This occurs when the letter form has become a single horizontal line.

Sharp A thin or fine pen stroke.

Simplified A type of writing where only the essential strokes are present.

Size How big or small the handwriting is; also see "relative" or "absolute."

Slant The slope of the writing.

Stroke The ink trail left by the pen on the paper.

Style How the strokes vary from the copybook taught, for example neglected, simplified, or enriched.

Suspended This occurs when the second downstroke in a letter does not reach the baseline; it is left hanging, suspended in the air.

Wavy line baseline An imaginary line at the bottom of each line of handwriting that runs across the page in an undulating way.

Wavy line letter form This occurs when the downstrokes in the letter "n" have become one wavy line instead of two vertical lines.

Width The broadness of the writing.

Word spacing Spacing seen between the words.

Zones Three zones make up the full size in the writing. The upper zone comprises the ascenders in letters such as "h" and "b," the lower zone is found in letters such as "g" and "y." The middle part of the letters is called the middle zone.

PERSONALITY TRAITS

a

adaptable light pressure, mixed slant, garland letter forms

adventurous right slant, rising baselines, irregular

alone, needs time to be left slant, wide word spacing, small size

analytical sharp, simplified, upright slant

articulate wide line spaces, irregular, clear layout

artistic arrhythmic, mixed slant, irregular, thick pen stroke

aspirations dominant upper zone, enriched style, wide line spaces

b

balanced mind regular, upright slant, balanced zones, rhythm

broad-minded thick pen stroke, broad width, right slant

bustling close word spaces, close line spaces, large size

c

calm rhythm, arcade letter forms, upright slant

careful narrow width, small size, thin pen stroke

cautious left slant, wide word spaces, small size

chatty close word spaces, garland letter forms, large size

challenge, can rise to rising baselines, heavy pressure, simplified

colorful thick pen stroke, large size, broad width, enriched style

committed narrow width, thin pen stroke, angle letter forms, stable baselines

common sense prevails stable baselines, upright slant, mix of angle and garland letter forms

concentration, sustained small size, narrow width, connected, stable baselines

consistent rhythm, regularity, arcade letter forms

controlled regularity, angle letter forms, narrow width

courageous right slant, heavy pressure, rising baselines

creative wavy baselines, disconnected, irregular

d

design, flair for enriched style, irregular, thick pen stroke

detail, eye for small size, legibility, simplified

determination angle letter forms, heavy pressure, rising baselines

diligent narrow width, stable baseline, thin pen stroke

disciplined regularity, heavy pressure, small size

e

easygoing garlands, thick pen stroke, broad width

economical narrow writing, angle letter forms, light pressure

emotional wavy baselines, irregular, arrhythmic, mixed slant, disconnected

empathetic garland letter forms, right slant, rhythmic

energetic heavy pressure, rising baselines, dominant lower zone

enterprising broad width, rising baselines, heavy pressure

enthusiasm large size, irregularity, broad width

ethical thin pen stroke, balanced zones, simplified

excitable arrhythmic, irregular, broad width

exhausted falling baselines, light pressure, widening left margin

f

factual, sticks to essentials simplified style, upright slant, stable baselines

family values important narrow left margins, left slant, thick pen stroke

far-sighted wide line spaces, dominant upper zone, broad width, large size

flexible wavy line letter forms, light pressure, mixed slant, broad width

friendly garland letter forms, broad width, thick pen stroke

future, keen to go forward right slant, narrow right margins, rising baselines

g

generous large size, thick pen stroke, broad width

h

happy rising baselines, broad width, irregular

hopes dominant upper zone, rising baseline, right slant

i

ideals dominant upper zone, simplified style, stable baselines

imaginative wavy baselines, disconnected, large size, irregularity

impulsive irregularity, right slant, broad width

individualist arrhythmic, irregular, disconnected

industrious angle letter forms, heavy pressure, connected

initiative large size, broad width, clear spaces between words and lines

instinctual drives dominant lower zone, heavy pressure, enriched style

intense small size, connected, regular

interests, lots of arrhythmic, irrregular, disconnected

i

job and home well balanced upright slant, mix of angle and garland letter forms, rhythmic

jobs, can do several mixed slant, disconnected, irregular

l

laid-back broad width, irregular, large size

level-headed upright slant, clear line spacing, mix of angle and garland letter forms

lists, makes wide spaces between lines, arcade letter forms, upright slant

lively large size, irregular, broad width

lives in the present dominant middle zone, upright slant, garland letter forms, disconnected

logical thinker connected, upright slant, thin pen stroke

loyal left slant, stable baselines, rhythmic

lucid thinker wide spaces between lines, simplified style, stable baseline

m

mediator wavy line letter forms, upright slant, firm pressure

methodical regularity, simplified, wide word spaces

modesty small size, simplified, stable baselines

multiskilled mixed slant, irregularity, broad width

musical rhythmic, wide word spacing, broad width

o

objective simplified style, upright slant, balanced zones

one-to-one contact, prefers wide word spacing, right slant, small size

optimistic rising baselines, right slant, broad width

options, likes to keep open wavy line letter forms, wavy baseline, irregular, disconnected

orderly wide line spaces, regularity, arcade letter forms

organizer wide word spaces, simplified style, heavy pressure

original cause, finds connected, dominant lower zone, simplified

ornaments and pictures, likes enriched style, thick pen stroke, irregularity

overworked falling baselines, light pressure, disconnected

p

past experiences for decision-making narrow left margins, left slant, arcade letter forms

past, leaves it behind wide left margins, right slant, dominant upper zone

patient rhythmic, garland letter forms, broad width

personal security is important dominant lower zone, left slant, connected

planning, good at wide line spaces, simplified style, heavy pressure

practical stable baselines, upright slant, dominant middle zone

precision small size, simplified, connected

prioritizes actions wide word spaces, irregular, simplified

projects, good at starting convex baselines, right slant, rising baselines

protective arcade letter forms, left slant, heavy pressure

r

refinement, likes thin pen stroke, simplified, upright slant

reflective left slant, narrow width, small size

reliable concave baselines, copybook style, heavy pressure, stable baselines

reserved wide word spacing, small size, left slant

resourceful broad width, irregular, firm pressure

rules, good at following copybook style, regularity, connected

s

scientific simplified style, upright slant, connected

secretive left slant, arcade letter forms, small size

selective wide word spaces, simplified, left slant

self-assured wide line spaces, balanced zones, rhythmic

self-controlled regularity, stable baselines, heavy pressure

self-disciplined stable baselines, upright slant, heavy pressure

senses are important thick pen stroke, enriched style, right slant

sensible rhythmic, upright slant, mix of angle and garland letter forms

sensitive arrhythmic, thin pen stroke, light pressure

single-minded regularity, connected, narrow width

sociable right slant, close word spaces, dominant middle zone

specialist small size, connected, upright slant

spontaneous close line and word spaces, irregular, right slant

strength heavy pressure, connected, stable baseline

stressed falling baselines, arrhythmic, disconnected

t

talent of a genius arrhythmic, irregular, broad width

tasks, will complete connected, concave baselines, angle letter forms

teams, enjoys working in copybook style, regularity, garland letter forms

tenacious narrow width, connected, heavy pressure

tender light pressure, thick pen stroke, garland letter forms

thorough concave baselines, wide line spaces, heavy pressure

thoughts, quick and plentiful neglected style, irregular, disconnected

tolerant rhythmic, garland letter forms, broad width

tradition, loves arcade letter forms, copybook style, regularity

trusting close word spaces, mingled line spaces, enriched style

u

uncertainty (temporary) wide right margins, disconnected, falling baselines

v

variety, enjoys irregularity, mixed slant, disconnected

vitality thick pen stroke, heavy pressure, rising baselines

w

warm-hearted right slant, close word spaces, garland letter forms

well-meaning close spaces between words and lines, enriched style

INDEX

ACKNOWLEDGMENTS

I would very much like to thank my parents, Peter and Joy Tew, for their help, especially for working with an initiative, thoroughness, and speed that I am unable to match. I would also like to thank my sister Maureen Tew and a few wonderful friends: Maureen Butterfield, Jim Ives, and Christopher and Veronika Strong, who were all supportive and helpful in their special ways. Finally I would like to thank my editor Rowan Davies for her patience, kindness, understanding, and help.

PICTURE ACKNOWLEDGMENTS

GettyOne Stone 78t, 146t, 150t, 154t, 158t, 162t, 174t, 178t, 182t; **Images Color Library** 79t, 170; **Superstock** 166t